BLACKS IN CLASSICAL MUSIC

Other Books By Raoul Abdul

Famous Black Entertainers of Today
The Magic of Black Poetry
Three Thousand Years of Black Poetry
(with Alan Lomax)

BLACKS
IN CLASSICAL MUSIC

A Personal History

By RAOUL ABDUL

DODD, MEAD & COMPANY
NEW YORK

Acknowledgment is made to the Weintraub Music Company for permission to reprint excerpts from the Short Symphony and the Suite for Piano and Cello, both by Howard Swanson, copyright 1951 by the Weintraub Music Company, New York, New York.

Excerpt from "Mother to Son" by Langston Hughes reprinted by permission of Harold Ober Associates Incorporated. Copyright 1926 by Alfred A. Knopf, Inc. Renewed.

ML
385
·A 27

1 2 3 4 5 6 7 8 9 10

Library of Congress Cataloging in Publication Data

Abdul, Raoul.
    Blacks in classical music.

    Includes index.
    1. Musicians, Black—Biography. I. Title.
ML385.A27   780'.92'2 [B]   77-11645
ISBN 0-396-07394-8

TO THE MEMORY OF ROLAND HAYES
AND TO
RICHARD MAYER HABER

Acknowledgments

I should like to express my gratitude to the editors of the newspapers that have provided a forum for me to express my ideas about music and musicians over a period of twenty-seven years.

Charles Loeb, city editor of the *Cleveland Call* and *Post*, took me under his personal supervision when I was an eighteen-year-old kid fresh out of high school. He guided my early steps through rewrites, obituaries, *and* music reviews.

Alfred Duckett, executive editor of the *New York Age*, appointed me music critic on the recommendation of Langston Hughes. He later arranged for my column, "The Cultural Scene," to be syndicated nationally by the Associated Negro Press.

James Hicks, executive editor of the *New York Amsterdam News*, appointed me music critic. Hicks, Publisher John Procope, and his assistant, Lucia Robinson, have stood behind my editorial views with fierce loyalty.

Contents

IV KEYBOARD ARTISTS

V INSTRUMENTALISTS

VI CONDUCTORS, ORCHESTRAS, AND
CHORUSES

VII DIVERTISSEMENTS

VIII ATTITUDES

Illustrations

Introduction

Until recently, the Black contribution to what is known as classical (read: European) music has remained in a kind of cultural closet. Actually, by 1881 there had been enough activity in this area to fill the pages of James M. Trotter's remarkable book *Music and Some Highly Musical People* (Boston: Lee and Shepard, 1881).

He chronicled the careers of such people as the soprano Elizabeth Taylor-Greenfield (1809–1876), known as "the Black Swan." During her brief career, she sang before Queen Victoria in England, toured our Eastern states, and attracted the attention of major music critics of the day.

Another figure to emerge was Justin Holland (1819–1886), whose instruction manuals for guitar became musts among enthusiasts for that instrument. His published works included *Holland's Comprehensive Method for the Guitar* (1874) and *Holland's Modern Method for Guitar* (1876).

The first Black concert pianist to gain recognition was Thomas Greene Bethune (1849–1908), known as "Blind Tom." This prodigy performed here and abroad in the true American Barnum and Bailey circus style, but contemporary accounts lead us to believe that his playing was of the highest caliber.

Although he was a native of Cuba and made his career primarily in Europe, the violinist José White (1839–1890) gained recognition in the United States when he appeared with the New York Philharmonic playing the Mendelssohn Concerto in E Minor in 1875.

Another pioneering effort was the Colored American Opera Company, which gave performances of Eichberg's *The Doctor of Alcantara* in Washington, D.C., and Philadelphia, Pa. in 1873. It received enthusiastic reviews from the daily press and proved that blacks could excel in the field of opera.

The great Czech composer Antonin Dvŏrák focused attention on the use of Black folk music as the basis of symphonic composition. But, it was the 1904, 1906, and 1910 visits here of the Black English composer Samuel Coleridge-Taylor (1875–1912) that inspired American Blacks to become serious composers.

When the tenor Roland Hayes (1887–1977) made his historic Town Hall debut in 1923, Blacks were recognized for the first time on the major concert stages of the United States. He eventually became one of the world's greatest *Lieder* interpreters and remains to this day a source of inspiration to singers.

The first Black American composer to have a symphonic work performed by a major American orchestra was William Grant Still (b. 1895). His *Afro-American* Symphony received its premiere in 1931 with the Rochester Philharmonic under Howard Hanson, and it remains a classic in the repertory.

At this point, it should be noted that Still's opera based on a libretto by Langston Hughes, *Troubled Island*, was the first by a Black to be performed by a major company. It was premiered in 1949 by the New York City Opera under Laszlo Halasz in honor of the company's fifth anniversary.

The first Black woman to appear in a leading role with a major American opera company was Caterina Jarboro when she played the title role in *Aida* with the Chicago Opera at the New York Hippodrome in 1933 before a capacity audience. This extraordinary soprano also excelled as a recitalist.

It was not until 1946 that a Black singer was engaged as a regular artist with a major American company. This was Todd Duncan, who made his debut as Tonio in *Pagliacci* with the New York City Opera. Soprano Camilla Williams followed shortly after in the title role in *Madama Butterfly*.

The first Black composer to win the New York Music Critics' Circle Award (1952) for the best symphonic work performed during the past season was Howard Swanson (b. 1907). His *Short* Symphony was premiered by the New York Philharmonic under Dimitri Mitropoulos at the November 23-24, 1950, concerts.

It remained for contralto Marian Anderson to open the doors of the Metropolitan Opera to Black singers. This historical occasion took place on January 7, 1955, when Miss Anderson played the role of Ulrica in *The Masked Ball*. Baritone Robert McFerrin and soprano Mattiwilda Dobbs followed immediately.

When pianist Andre Watts made his spectacular appearance on January 31, 1963, with the New York Philharmonic under Leonard Bernstein, he became the first Black instrumental superstar. His way had been paved by Hazel Harrison, Natalie Hinderas, George Walker, Eugene Haynes, and others.

Founded by a committee of twelve Black and two non-Black musicians in 1964, the Symphony of the New World remains the only major predominantly Black orchestra in the United States. As of 1977, it was giving its twelfth season of concerts. Its musical director is Everett Lee, a Black conductor.

The first Black permanent conductor of a major American orchestra was Henry Lewis, who was appointed to the New Jersey Symphony in 1968. He later became the first Black conductor at the Metropolitan Opera, and he is still a member of the musical staff of that company.

Paving the way for Lewis was Dean Dixon (1915–1976), who was the first Black to make a career as a conductor of symphonic music. Dixon held the post of musical director with the Göteborg Symphony (Sweden), the Hessischer Rundfunk Orchestra (Germany), and the Sydney Symphony Orchestra. (Australia).

In the realm of music criticism, only two writers have held posts with major "white" newspapers. One of these was Collins George, who until recently wrote for the *Detroit Free Press*. Another was Carman Moore, who wrote for several years for the *Village Voice*.

The late Nora Holt, once music critic for the *Amsterdam News*, was the only Black member of the New York Music Critics Circle and Dr. Gladys Graham was a member of the board of the Music Critics Association. Both of these women deserve special credit for their pioneering efforts.

These are some of the "firsts." Over the years, many outstanding talents have appeared in the musical galaxy. Like rockets on the Fourth of July, some have exploded into a magnificent display after which they disappeared into oblivion. Some have endured. This book is a record of their ascent.

I
COMPOSERS

1   A Chevalier Rediscovered

Even the folks downtown celebrated Negro History
Week. Under the direction of Newell Jenkins, Clarion Concerts wound up its Town Hall series with a *Symphonie
Concertante* for Two Violins and Orchestra by the Mulatto
composer Chevalier de Saint-Georges (1739–1799) and other
works.

Born in Guadeloupe (West Indies) of an African mother
and the governor of the island, Saint-Georges was sent to
Paris at the age of thirteen to be educated like any other
member of the upper classes.

Under the guidance of the great French violin master Leclair, Saint-Georges acquired a mastery of that instrument
comparable to the best of his day. He studied composition
under Gossec and turned out operas, concertos, and sym-

NOTE: In many instances, chapters begin with a quotation,
slightly updated, of a review that I have written in the
past concerning the subject. The source and date of
such reviews are indicated in footnotes at the back of
the book.

phonies of a high caliber. He was a fascinating character and, it is also said, an outstanding swordsman, a brilliant conversationalist, and altogether the darling of French society.

In the first performance since the eighteenth century, Jenkins and soloists Gerald Tarack and Alan Martin gave Saint-Georges' *Symphonie Concertante* a beautifully balanced reading that brought out the inherent charm of the score. What it lacks in originality is more than compensated for by the skill with which it is constructed.[1]

To be young, gifted, and Black in Paris on the eve of the French Revolution must have been most exciting indeed for Le Chevalier de Saint-Georges. But even more significant is the fact this remarkable young man took his musical gift and developed it to the point that he became the first major Black figure in the world of what is known as classical music.

Because he gained so much celebrity during his lifetime, Saint-Georges became the subject of a four-volume biographical novel entitled *Le Chevalier de Saint-Georges* by Roger de Beauvoir (Paris: Calmann-Levy, 1838). Highly romanticized and alternating precariously between fact and fantasy, this novel has unfortunately been used as source material for many articles and papers on the composer.

Using the Beauvoir novel as a source, Black historian J. A. Rogers wrote of Saint-Georges:

> He was the most dazzling and fascinating figure at the most splendid court of Europe; as a violinist, pianist, poet, musical composer and actor, he was phenomenal; as a swordsman he so far eclipsed the best of his time and in his prime none could

match him; as a marksman none could pull a trigger with such unerring aim; as a soldier and commander he performed prodigious feats on the field of battle; as a dancer, swimmer, horseman, and skater, he was the most graceful in a land supreme for its grace and elegance; in the matter of dress, he was the model of his day, setting the fashions in England and France; a king of France, a future king of England, and royal princes sought his company, and to crown all he possessed a spirit of rare generosity, kindliness and rectitude.

One of the more accurate accounts of the life and works of Saint-Georges to appear in this country was an article entitled "The Chevalier De Saint-George" by Lionel De La Laurencie (translated by Frederick H. Martens from the original French), published in *Musical Quarterly*, Boston, in January of 1919. More recently, Dr. Barry S. Brook has written well-researched articles for encyclopedias and made some of Saint-Georges' scores available through the publication in 1962 in Paris of his three-volume series *La Symphonie Francaise dans la seconde moitie du XVIIIe siècle.*

According to such contemporary eighteenth-century sources as the *Mercure de France*, Saint-Georges first emerged on the major musical scene during the season of 1772–1773 when he appeared as soloist in two of his own concertos for principal violin and orchestra at the Concerts des Amateurs, which were founded by his teacher, Gossec. His first published works were six string quartets, which came out in 1773 under the auspices of Sieber. It was also in this same year that Gossec turned over his post as director of the Concerts des Amateurs to Saint-Georges when he (Gossec) moved on to the more prestigious Concerts Spirituels in the Tuileries. It is obvious that Gossec had great confidence in the musical abilities of his protégé.

In June of 1775, the publishing house of Bailleux brought out a series of concertos for violin by Saint-Georges; by the end of that same year, he had completed a collection of *symphonies concertantes.* One of the latter works was featured on Christmas day at the Concerts Spirituels, the highest honor a composer of that day could achieve.

Saint-Georges was also drawn to the theater, and in July of 1777 he presented a comedy in three acts interspersed with music under the title *Ernestine* at the Comedie Italienne. He became a favorite in the circle of the Duke of Orleans and was appointed to a post in the noble's hunting establishment, which lasted until the duke's death in 1785. He continued to turn out more works for the theater, such as *La Chasse* (1778), *L'Amant Anonyme* (1780), *La Fille Garçon* (1787), and *La Marchand de Marrons* (1788).

According to the *Archives Historiques du Ministere de la Guerre*, in 1791 Saint-Georges became chief of brigade of a regiment of black men called the American Hussars. Because of his earlier association with the Duke of Orleans, Louis-Philippe (1725–1785) as well as his successor "Philippe-Egalite," it is not at all surprising that he soon fell under suspicion of disloyalty leading to dismissal and jail in 1793. Eventually he proved his innocence, was briefly reinstated to his post, then again removed. Nothing was heard of him again until his death around June 12, 1799. In his book *Bruchstuecke einer Reise durch Frankreich in Fruehling und Sommer*, E. M. von Arndt wrote:

> In all the theatres, promenades, cafes and gardens resounded the name of the great Saint-Georges. In the streets they stopped to exchange the news. For three or four days his name echoed in all the newspapers. They lauded his skill in all the arts, his fine manner, his force, his generosity and gaiety.

An excellent sampling of the music by Saint-Georges can be heard on Columbia's Black Composer Series, Volume 1. Included are *Symphonie Concertante* in G Major (Opus 13), Symphony No. 1 in G Major (Opus 11, No. 1), Scene from *Ernestine*, and String Quartet No. 1 in C Major (Opus 1, No. 1). Performers include the London Symphony Orchestra under Paul Freeman; Miriam Fried and Jaime Laredo, violinists; Faye Robinson, soprano; and the Juilliard Quartet.

The noted musicologist Dr. Dominique-Rene de Lerma is in the process of preparing performance editions of the works of Saint-Georges. I had the privilege of hearing one of his adaptations of a Sonata for Flute and Harp, rearranged for Flute, Cello, and Piano, at Lincoln University. It was performed quite beautifully by Antoinette Handy's Trio Pro Viva.

2   Creoles, Negroes, and Gottschalk

A Creole, according to *The American College Dictionary*, (New York: Random House, 1947) is: "(in Louisiana and elsewhere) born in the region but of French ancestry." Note also: "a person of mixed Creole and Negro ancestry speaking a form of French or Spanish."

The United States Bureau of the Census has ruled thusly: "A person of mixed white and Negro blood should be returned as a Negro, no matter how small the percentage of

Negro blood. Both black and mulatto persons are to be returned as Negroes, without distinction."

With this knowledge in mind, one can discuss Louis Moreau Gottschalk (1829–1869), a Creole who became the first American-born pianist and composer to gain international fame. For many years, there have been some rather persistant rumors that he had that powerful drop of Black blood.

Gottschalk was born in New Orleans, where it is known that official records have been tampered with to suit the conceits of certain well-connected families. Most sources now say that his father was an English-born Jew of Spanish origin and his mother was descended from French aristocracy.

Dr. Robert E. Peterson (M.D.) of Philadelphia, who was married to one of Gottschalk's sisters, even denied the Jewish claim and insisted that the composer's father was an Englishman and that his mother was a Creole of noble origin. Could there be a "dark" secret in the closet?

"Passing" is a very popular pastime, as any bona fide Black citizen of these United States can bear witness. Many has been the Black grandmother who proudly sits in the kitchen while her own flesh and blood masquerades behind a White mask in the parlor. The Cuban Mulatto poet Nicolas Guillen wrote:

> Yesterday they called me "nigger"
> so I should get mad;
> but he who called me thus
> was as Black as I am.
> You pretend to be so white—
> but I know your grandmother!

All of these thoughts raced through my mind when I recently discovered a recording *The World of Louis Moreau Gottschalk* (Vanguard 723/724). It contains a healthy sampling of his composing efforts, performed by pianists Eugene List and Reid Nibley, who are assisted by the Utah Symphony Orchestra.

Included on the recording are several of Gottschalk's compositions that draw upon his childhood memories of Creole and Negro melodies. "The Banjo" quotes "The Camptown Races" as well as "Mister Banjo," and "Bamboula" uses cakewalk rhythms. "La Savane" reflects shades of "Lolette."

This fine recording also includes his piano solo "The Last Hope." When it was republished in the 1860s, it sold 35,000 copies within a few years and went through twenty-eight editions.

As a concert pianist, Gottschalk attracted the attention of Chopin, who said to him, "My child, I predict that you will become the king of pianists." Years later, he returned to New York City to give eighty concerts in one season. It is time to open the racial closet and let the light shine in.[2]

Besides a number of short piano pieces, Gottschalk also wrote a Grand Tarantella for Piano and Orchestra (Opus 67), *A Night in the Tropics* (1859), a cantata, two unproduced operas, and other short symphonic works. His superbly written diary, *Notes of a Pianist*, offers interesting insights into his life and times.

3   Coleridge-Taylor: 100 Years Later

"What Brahms has done for the Hungarian folk-music, Dvořák for the Bohemian, and Grieg for the Norwegian, I have tried to do for these Negro melodies." Thus wrote Samuel Coleridge-Taylor in the foreword to his *Twenty-four Negro Melodies Transcribed for Piano* (1904).

More than any other composer, Coleridge-Taylor was the greatest source of inspiration to the Black musicians of the United States. And in 1975, he was honored on the centennial of his birth by celebrations in Atlanta, New York, and elsewhere.

Born in London on August 15, 1875, he was the son of an African father and an English mother. Following his training at the Royal College of Music, he went on to achieve world acclaim as a composer. His cantata *Hiawatha* is performed annually in England. He died on September 1, 1912.

One source of his Black awareness is revealed in a letter to Andrew Hilyer of Washington, D.C., dated January 3, 1904. It begins: "This is only a line to thank you over and over again for so kindly sending me the book by Mr. Du Bois. It is the finest book I have ever read by a coloured man . . ."

A letter to him dated June 1, 1903, is self-explanatory. It began: "My Dear Sir—At a meeting of the Board of Managers of the S. Coleridge-Taylor Choral Society, I was directed to convey its invitation to you to visit Washington and personally conduct one or more presentations of your immortal *Hiawatha*."

This resulted in his first visit to the United States in 1904. He described his arrival thusly: "When I stepped off the boat at Boston there were half a dozen newspaper men waiting to devour me." Indeed, his handsome face beamed from the pages of every morning paper the next day.

The Coleridge-Taylor Festival, as it was called, occupied two evenings in Washington and a third in Baltimore. The first event, devoted entirely to *Hiawatha*, was on November 16th in Convention Hall. The soloists were Estella Clough, Arthur J. Freeman, and Harry T. Burleigh.

The Georgia Baptist reported, "When Samuel Coleridge-Taylor of London, walked upon the platform of Convention Hall last Wednesday night, and made his bow to four thousand people, the event marked an epoch in the history of the Negro race of the world."

He was received in the homes of many distinguished people during his stay. But the climax of his visit was when he was received by President Teddy Roosevelt at the White House. After a long conversation, during which they exchanged sentiments of mutual admiration, the President presented Coleridge-Taylor with an autographed portrait.

Many years later, when his Clarinet Quintet was performed at the 1972 Newport Music Festival, the *New York Times* wrote, "It is an assured piece of writing in the post-Romantic tradition, sweetly melodic without being cloying, sometimes with a powerful thrust and beautifully written for the five players."

This is a fair evaluation of this particular piece and might apply to his entire output. He was a naturally musical person out of whom flowed original melodies as easily as most of us breathe. He was a fine craftsman, too. But, most of all, he served as an inspiration to all Black musicians to come.

In the United States there were only two major celebrations of Coleridge-Taylor's centennial. The first was the annual Afro-American Music Workshop at Atlanta University, during which I was invited to sing a group of his songs for voice and piano. The second was a pre-centenary concert by the Triad Chorale assisted by the Schubert Music Society at Alice Tully Hall in New York City. My efforts to get the music editor of the *New York Times* to do a feature was met with marked indifference.

4   Jazz with a Ph.D.

With the exception of one work, a program offered by the Symphony of the New World at Carnegie Hall might have been entitled "Jazz with a Ph.D." Dr. William Grant Still's *Afro-American* Symphony was contrasted with jazz originals featuring the Jimmy Owens Quartet.

Opening the program, the Still work holds the distinction of being the first symphony written by a Black American. Since its premiere in 1931 by the Rochester Philharmonic under Dr. Howard Hanson, it has been performed by major orchestras throughout the world.

Because it became a classic, its themes might strike one as being a bit "corny" (as the *Times* put it). This is also true of Dvořak's Symphony *From the New World*, which I heard the Cleveland Orchestra play in the same hall.

Still's work, which is masterfully orchestrated in this 1969 revision, is in my opinion the most successful attempt to date of incorporating jazz into a symphonic form. Conductor Everett Lee lavished great attention to minute details in the score and the result was a superb performance.

Although not written by a Black composer, Walter Piston's finely crafted Concerto for Viola and Orchestra (1957) provided an excellent vehicle for displaying the talents of violist Dr. Marcus Thompson. His vibrant tone, fine musicianship, and ingratiating personality won an ovation from the large audience.

Dr. Thompson, who is one of the nation's few Black solo violists, has appeared with the National Symphony in Washington, D.C., the Boston Pops, Marlboro Festival, and Spoleto Festival. He is also Professor of Humanities at the Massachusetts Institute of Technology.

Following the intermission, the program featured "Never Subject to Change," "The Jazz Jaleo," "Do-It-To-It" by Jimmie Owens and an arrangement of "Come Sunday" by Duke Ellington. In these works, the Jimmy Owens Quartet joined the full orchestra in a kind of symphonic jam session.

Each work featured Owens on either the trumpet or flugelhorn, and the results were electrifying. I found myself wishing that the Quartet would play alone without the symphony orchestra. Jazz is an art in itself, in no need of embellishment. But, it was interesting to hear a little "jazz with a Ph.D." [3]

William Grant Still, born in Woodville, Mississippi, on May 11, 1895, is known as the Dean of Black Composers. His *Afro-American* Symphony (1931) is the first major symphony by a Black composer in the United States and has become a classic. His *Troubled Island* (1938), with libretto by Langston Hughes, is the first opera by a Black composer to be performed by a major company (New York City Opera,

1949). He also holds the distinction of being the first Black to conduct a major symphony orchestra. The noted conductor Dr. Leon Thompson chose as the subject of his doctoral dissertation "A Historical and Stylistic Analysis of the Music of William Grant Still and a Thematic Catalogue of his Works." The following is an interview with Dr. Thompson.

Abdul: Since you were permitted to do the research for your thesis in the home of Dr. Still, you must have gotten to know him quite well. What is he like as a person?

Thompson: I remember him as a very strong person inwardly who gave the outward impression of being a warm, almost meek individual. Actually, he was not meek, but quite strong and adamant about the things in which he believed. He is very lucid in terms of expressing his own ideas, and he can expound on almost any subject, not just music.

Abdul: What is the place of William Grant Still within the context of the whole American musical scene?

Thompson: I think that he is unique, and I think history will deal with him very well because of his uniqueness. I think that any evaluation of his output must be considered from the viewpoint of three distinct periods.

Abdul: Could you elaborate on those periods?

Thompson: In the beginning, when he first started, he was experimenting. That, to me, was the most exciting period of his life, but his music was completely castrated by the critics at that time, as was the music of Varese and anyone else who was doing anything out of the ordinary. Being Black in a white society and trying to gain acceptance for himself as a person and for his music caused him to bow to the wishes of some of the critics and his advisers. So we see that he moved into a second period, in which most of his works carried a Black theme (at that time called a Negro theme). This was a time when he wrote *And They Lynched*

Him on a Tree and the *Sahdji* ballet. After that period was over, he began to think that "now that I've said something in terms of experimentation and I've said something in terms of my own roots, I now want to speak in general about music. I'll say what I want to say."

Abdul: What would you say are the most significant works of each period?

Thompson: I don't think that we can speak of the first period, because he destroyed most of the manuscripts. His major works come from the second period. The *Afro-American* Symphony, *In Darker America* and *Sahdji* and the opera *Troubled Island* came out of this period. The third has some very interesting works as well. His *Poem for Orchestra* (commissioned by the Cleveland Orchestra) is characteristic of this period. And, of course, the opera *Highway No. 1 U.S.A.*

Abdul: When I hear works of this period, I find it impossible to pinpoint his Blackness.

Thompson: That is intentional. It is my opinion that his wife, Verna Arvey, had some influence on his thinking at that time. Be that as it may, his skill as a composer is very evident throughout the second and third periods. Whatever he set out to do, he did very well.

Abdul: When Dr. Still's opera *Troubled Island* received its world premiere in 1949 by the New York City Opera, the reviews were quite mixed. What are your reactions to the score?

Thompson: I think that, for the first opera, it shows a great deal of strength in operatic writing. You have to stop and consider that Verdi and Puccini wrote many operas before *La Forza del Destino* and *La Boheme* came along. It contains typical romantic music. There is nothing especially unusual about it, but it is beautifully done, well-executed operatic writing.

Abdul: Right now there is a big push towards establishing a real American lyric theater, a place where native works can find a forum. Do you feel that the operas of Dr. Still will someday take their place in the standard repertory of such a company?

Thompson: I don't know how important a part they will play, but they certainly deserve consideration. They are very worthwhile, and they should be seen and heard so that they can stand on their own merit. You can't evaluate them unless you play them.

Abdul: Are there any special considerations to take into account when a conductor approaches a work by Dr. Still?

Thompson: I approach his music in the same manner as I would that of any other composer. When I approach Dvořák, I try to find something of its Slavic nature. With Bartók, I do the same thing. There are certain stylistic things unique to each composer that I seek out. I am interested in what the music has to say, what it means to me, and how I can bring out the things that I know the composer is trying to say to his public.

5   Fela Sowande's Seventieth Birthday

When the works of Nigerian composer Fela Sowande were played in 1962 in Carnegie Hall, New Yorkers had their first opportunity to hear music in the European classical tradition by an African. This historic moment was distinguished by the presence of many leading African diplomats.

Highlighting the program were two orchestral works entitled *African* Suite and *A Folk Symphony*. In his review in the *New York Times*, Alan Rich pointed out: "The way he incorporates native tunes into large forms and his harmonic vocabulary quite strongly suggests Ralph Vaughan Williams."

One Sunday afternoon, Saint Philip's Church devoted its twentieth annual Festival of Sacred Music to choral and organ works by Dr. Sowande in honor of his seventieth birthday. The performers included the choir, soloists, and choirmaster and organist Dr. Eugene W. Hancock.

It was interesting to hear the treatment by an African of many familiar Afro-American spirituals. Surprisingly enough, the results seemed somewhat square. The organ works showed more originality and compositional skill, due in great part to the fine playing by Dr. Hancock.

Dr. Sowande, who is currently teaching at the University of Pittsburgh, was introduced to the large audience toward the end of the program. The church's rector, the Reverend Dr. M. Moran Weston delivered a moving address under the title "In Celebration of Music." [4]

Fela Sowande, born in Oyo, Nigeria, May 29, 1905, was educated at C.M.S. Grammar School and King's College in Lagos. He also studied at London University and Trinity College of Music. He is a fellow of the Royal College of Organists and Trinity College of Music.

Dr. Sowande has had his compositions played by members of the New York Philharmonic, The B.B.C. Symphony, and his works have been included in the Columbia Records Black Composers Series. His most widely heard piece is *African* Suite, in five movements for string orchestra and harp.

6   The Black Experience in Sound

There is a commercial on one of our radio stations that boasts that its fare represents "the total Black experience in sound." This motto came to mind as I listened to an annual Black History Week concert offered by the Symphony of the New World at Carnegie Hall.

Howard Swanson's *Short* Symphony (1948), which opened the program, represents the Black musical experience in its most sophisticated form. In it, the threads of "Negritude" have been so subtly woven into a fabric of such beauty that it must be given the place of honor to be appreciated. Its placement on this occasion is one of the reasons that its special magic failed to work. Another, is that the orchestra was not up to its demands. But, more important, conductor Leon Thompson did not seem to understand exactly what the score was all about.

William Grant Still's *From a Lost Continent*, on the other hand, came off quite well. Thompson, a specialist in this composer's works, led the orchestra and the unusually fine Howard University Choir in a performance that brought out the best of this conservative, but finely wrought score.

Of special interest was the world premiere of Noel Da Costa's *Ceremony of Spirituals*. Its thematic material is drawn from three Afro-American spirituals, and its three movements are brought together by improvisational interludes featuring a saxophone or soprano soloist.

Although it seemed a bit long, the work has been very skill-

fully put together by its composer. It was quite well performed by all the forces, but special mention should go to
soprano Barbara Grant and saxophonist Sam Rivers. The
capacity audience received it with great enthusiasm.

Billy Taylor's Suite for Jazz Piano and Orchestra was a
series of improvisations with symphonic background. Featuring Taylor and his trio, each piece emerged polished and
gleaming, like those crystal champagne glasses that one finds
in an Upper East Side supper club.[5]

Howard Swanson, born in Atlanta in 1907, is without question the most distinguished living Black composer. He
studied at the Cleveland Institute of Music with Herbert
Elwell and in Paris with Nadia Boulanger. He has received
Rosenwald and Guggenheim fellowships and many grants,
including one from the Academy of Arts and Letters. He first
came to national attention when Marian Anderson sang one
of his songs in 1950. Under Dimitri Mitropoulos, the New
York Philharmonic on November 23, 1950, performed his
Short Symphony (1948), a work which subsequently received a citation by the New York Music Critics Circle in
1952. His major works include two more symphonies: *Night
Music* for chamber orchestra; pieces for cello and piano;
two piano sonatas; and many songs. Major orchestras and
solo performers throughout the world have performed his
music.

In November of 1971, I organized The Friends of Howard
Swanson for the purpose of presenting "The Music of How-
ard Swanson" at Carnegie Recital Hall in New York City.
Early in 1977, Morehouse College of the Atlanta University
Center devoted its annual Afro-American Music Workshop
to his works in honor of his seventieth birthday. The Honor-

able Maynard Jackson, mayor of Atlanta, issued a proclamation in his honor. This was followed in June of the same year by a special concert in his honor at Alice Tully Hall, New York City, under the auspices of Triad Presentations, Inc.

Before I discuss the music of Howard Swanson, I would like to look briefly into the meaning of the word *Negritude* as it is reflected in the works of contemporary French-speaking African and Caribbean poets. Senghor, Cesaire, and Damas all made their mark on the Paris Swanson knew.

The Black scholar Wilfred Cartey writes: "To return symbolically to the source, to abnegate the loss, the alienation, the confusion, will be the prime intention and motive of the Negritude poets as they search through their single selves for a communal African authenticity."

The poets of Negritude were placed in a situation where they had to express their Blackness in a language foreign to their cultural heritage. They not only mastered this language, but revitalized it by imposing on it their own special rhythmic and tonal characteristics. It is a triumph of their artistry.

For Howard Swanson, the symbolic return to the source is the blues, one of the cornerstones of the Afro-American musical heritage. He must express himself within the confines of the traditional European classical music language. Like the poets of Negritude, he enhances it with elements from his heritage.

His setting of Edwin Markham's poem "The Valley" is a case in point. There is nothing at all "Afro" or "Afro-American" in the text, and yet Swanson manages to see it through the eyes of an Afro-American and turn it into a Black experience.

❖   ❖   ❖

In the opening movement of his *Short* Symphony, the blues are ever present, even though they sometimes become seemingly lost in his contrapuntal gyrations:

Excerpt from "Short Symphonies"

And examine the opening movement of his Suite for Cello and Piano:

Excerpt from Suite for Cello and Piano

In an essay published in Budapest in 1931, Bela Bartok wrote: "Folk music will become a source of inspiration for a country's music only if the transplantation of its motifs is the work of a great creative talent." I am convinced that, for America, that genius is Howard Swanson.

There are several excellent performances of Swanson's music currently available on recordings. The *Short* Symphony is played by the Vienna State Opera Orchestra under the direction of Franz Litschauer on CRI-SD 254. His Seven Songs are superbly interpreted by soprano Helen Thigpen and pianist David Allen on Desto-DST 6422. And his recent Trio of Flute, Oboe and Piano is on Folkways-FTS 33903 (Volume 3, New American Music).

7   Ulysses Kay: New Horizons

"The youngest of our guests, Ulysses Kay, was represented in the concert by his overture 'Of New Horizons.' This
smallish work is testimony of the genuine artistic talent of
the composer." These words appeared in *Pravda* when the
Moscow State Radio Orchestra performed the piece in 1958.

This concert was part of a visit to the Soviet Union by four
American composers: Kay, Roy Harris, Peter Mennin, and
Roger Sessions. This visit was under the terms of the U.S.
State Department Cultural, Educational and Technical Ex-
change Agreement.

The Kay overture provided just the right tone to open a
concert at Carnegie Hall by the New Jersey Symphony. It is
bright, cheerful, conservative, and finely wrought. And it was
given an excellent performance by the orchestra under Irwin Hoffman.[6]

Ulysses Kay, born in 1917 in Tucson, Arizona, is the most
consistently played Black American composer. One reason
may be that he works within the broad European tradition.
Another, is the fact that his output is so varied that there is
a piece for every occasion.

He studied at the University of Arizona, the Eastman
School of Music, and worked with Otto Luening and Paul
Hindemith. He also spent several years in Italy on fellow-
ships. He has been serious music consultant at Broadcast

Music and Distinguished Professor of Music at Herbert H. Lehman College.

His large output includes chamber music, concertos, cantatas, symphonies, and three operas. His most recent opera is based on Margaret Walker's novel *Jubilee* and was recently premiered by Opera/South in Jackson, Mississippi. He has also been the recipient of several honorary doctorates.

When his *Markings* was premiered in 1966 by the Detroit Symphony under Sixten Ehrling, the *Detroit News* wrote: "There is an abundance of smoothly integrated solo writing, and Kay's flair for orchestra coloration, long a trademark, is unobtrusively brought into play when shifting rhythms threaten to fragment the thematic span."

8   George Walker's New Piece

Several major musical events prompted me to fly out to Cleveland, Ohio to check them out. One of these was the world premiere of George Walker's *Dialogus* for Violincello and Orchestra with the Cleveland Orchestra as a Bicentennial salute on Thursday, April 22, 1976.

The following Saturday evening, I rushed from my seat on the plane to a more comfortable one in Severance Hall just in time to hear the first notes of the new Walker piece which opened the program of the Cleveland Orchestra under its musical director Lorin Maazel and featuring cellist Stephen Gerber.

Commissioned by the Musical Arts Association, the work was sketched during the summer of 1975 at Lake Como in

Italy. The composer likens the solo cello at times to a "voice in the forest" surrounded by things that are not directly related to what it has to say.

Dialogus is the work of a very sophisticated musical personality. The cello writing is unusually fine, exploiting its technical possibilities to the limits, and the orchestration is skillfully put together. The remarkable teamwork between soloist and conductor made the piece "live." [7]

George Walker (b. 1922, Washington, D.C.) received his musical training at Oberlin College, Curtis Institute of Music, American Academy in Fontainebleau, and Eastman School of Music. He has had a distinguished career as a concert pianist, having received his training under Rudolf Serkin, Mieczyslaw Horszowski, Robert Casadesus, and others. He studied composition under Rosario Scalero, Gian Carlo Menotti, and Nadia Boulanger.

Among his awards are Fulbright, Whitney, MacDowell, Guggenheim, and Rockefeller fellowships. He has received commissions from the National Endowment, the Musical Arts Association (Cleveland, Ohio), and others. He has held teaching posts at the New School for Social Research, Smith College, University of Colorado, Rutgers University, and Peabody Institute of Music.

His works have been played by such major orchestras as the Cleveland Orchestra, the Minnesota Symphony, the Atlanta Symphony, the Detroit Symphony, and the Symphony of the New World. Some of his large works include Concerto for Trombone and Orchestra (Columbia Black Composers Series Recording), Lyric for Strings (also Columbia), and Piano Concerto. His piano sonatas are in the repertory of many outstanding artists including Natalie Hinderas,

Leon Bates, Frances Walker, Raymond Jackson, and Robert Jordan.

9   Hale Smith's *Rituals*

On Easter Sunday afternoon, April 18, 1976, the American Symphony Orchestra offered the New York premiere of Hale Smith's *Ritual and Incantations*. This piece was originally conducted by Paul Freeman in 1974 with the Houston Symphony and repeated this year with the Detroit Symphony.

The composer tells us "there are groupings of quintuplets, septuplets, rhythmic and textural overlays in uneven groupings that derive ultimately from West African traditions. . . ." From these few excerpts from the program notes, the reader has probably surmised that he is an intellectual composer.

In this sixteen-minute work, Smith has taken a musical idea and developed it into an artistic whole that both fascinates the listener's mind and his spirit. It is his ability to touch our emotions that makes him stand out from his contemporaries, and his efforts on this occasion were rewarded by three ovations.

Under the able direction of Kazuyoshi Akiyama, the program also included the Bach-Stokowski Fugue in G minor, which was played in honor of orchestra founder Leopold Stokowski's ninetieth birthday. The players brought everything vibrantly to life, and their playing still reflects the high standards set by the master.[8]

*   *   *

Hale Smith (b. 1925) grew up in Cleveland, Ohio, where he attended the Cleveland Institute of Music (M. Mus.). He has been on the teaching staff of C. W. Post College of Long Island University and is currently professor of music at the University of Connecticut at Storrs.

The first opportunity I had to hear a large part of his musical output was at an all-Smith program on a Sunday afternoon in 1955 at Karamu Theatre in Cleveland, Ohio. There were performances of his String Quartet, two groups of songs, and a Duo for Violin and Piano.

The latter work appealed to critic Herbert Elwell (*Cleveland Plain Dealer*), who wrote: "Of these works, the Duo (1953) proved the most vigorous and convincing writing, though in all of them one felt the impress of a musical mind of great sensitivity."

Since that time, Smith has taken his place as one of the most distinguished American composers. His *Contours* for orchestra (1961) was commissioned in 1960 by Broadcast Music, Inc., in celebration of its twentieth anniversary and premiered by the Louisville Orchestra on October 17, 1962.

Other works include: *In Memoriam—Beryl Rubenstein* (1953), with poems by Langston Hughes and Russell Atkins; Epicedial Variations for Violin and Piano (1956); Orchestral Set (1962); Music for Harp and Orchestra (1967); and numerous other works. His music has been recorded on Columbia and CRI.

10   Olly Wilson and Good Company

On April 5, 1968, Milton Babbitt, Vladimir Ussachev-sky, and George Balch Wilson went to Dartmouth College to judge the first competition devoted entirely to electronic music. Out of one hundred entries from around the world, they chose *Cetus* by Olly Woodrow Wilson as the winner.

Since that time, Dr. Wilson has received commissions from several orchestras. Through the assistance of the Martha Baird Rockefeller Fund for Music, Inc., and the Baltimore Symphony, his *Akwan* for piano, electric piano, amplified strings, and orchestra has been recorded (Columbia-M33434).

On Wednesday evening, February 23, 1977, at Carnegie Hall, the Boston Symphony offered the New York premiere of his *Voices* as part of a program which included Respighi's *Ancient Airs and Dances* and Rimsky-Korsakov's *Scheherazade*. This is not bad company at all for a thirty-nine-year-old composer.

In this work, Wilson uses a large orchestra, with amplified piano and double basses and several African instruments in addition to the regular percussion section. His command of his materials is masterful and the work holds our interest throughout. But, most of all, it is genuinely musical.[9]

Olly Wilson was born in 1937 in St. Louis, where he attended Washington University. He continued his studies at the University of Illinois, where he received a M. Mus. degree and at the State University of Iowa, where he earned a Ph.D. in composition. He studied electronic music at the Studio for Experimental Music in 1967 at the University of Illinois. He has played double bass with various orchestras and held teaching posts at Florida A. & M. College, West Virginia University, Indiana University, Oberlin College, and the University of California at Berkeley.

In addition to his 1968 Dartmouth Arts Council prize for *Cetus*, Wilson has had a Guggenheim Fellowship, a citation from The American Academy of Arts and Letters, and The National Institute of Arts and Letters. His works have been performed by the Boston Symphony, the Baltimore Symphony, the Atlanta Symphony, the Oakland Symphony, and others.

Among his more than thirty works, which include piano, chamber, ballet, songs, and choral compositions, are *Akwan* (for piano, electric piano, amplified strings, and orchestra) *In Memoriam Martin Luther King, Jr.* (for chorus and tape), *Piano Piece* (for piano and tape), and *Voices*. Several have been recorded by Columbia and Desto Records.

11 Folk Music in Symphonic Garb

Shortly before the premiere of his symphony *From the New World* (Opus 95) in 1893, Antonin Dvořák stated: "In the Negro melodies of America I discover all that is needed for a great and noble school of music." To this day, his work remains a shining example of how to use Negro folk material.

In an essay published in Budapest in 1931, Béla Bartók wrote: "Folk music will become a source of inspiration for a country's music only if the transplantation of its motifs is the work of a great creative talent." Bartók's own success in this area remains unsurpassed.

With this in mind, one can better appreciate the immensity of the task Noel Da Costa took on when he composed his *Ceremony of Spirituals* for soprano, saxophone, chorus, and orchestra. The results were heard recently at its premiere on Sunday, February 6, 1977 by the Symphony of the New World at Carnegie Hall.

Its three movements drew on Afro-American spirituals as thematic material for elaboration and motivic development. These included "You Hear the Lambs A-cryin'," "Lord, I Want Two Wings to Fly Away!", and "I'm Troubled in Mind." I also detected a short quote from "Round about the Mountain."

As I have stated elsewhere, the work has been very skillfully put together by its composer. But, for my taste, there were too many lengthy references to the folk material in pure unadulterated form. These had a power so great that they tended to negate Da Costa's own contribution.

In the second movement, the saxophonist is allowed to "shout against a sound background (short motifs sung and played freely by the chorus and orchestra.)" The effect was stunning and original and provided what Da Costa should have used as a focus of the entire piece.

The work was given a fine performance by the Symphony of the New World under the direction of Leon Thompson, in collaboration with the Howard University Choir. And special credit must be given to the soloists, soprano Barbara Grant and saxophonist Sam Rivers, both of whom were outstanding.[10]

Noel Da Costa (b. 1930) received his musical education at Queens College of City University of New York and Columbia University. While engaged in graduate studies at Columbia, he received the Seidl Fellowship in Composition. A few years later, he was awarded a Fulbright Fellowship to study in Florence, Italy, with Maestro Luigi Dallapiccola.

His works include: *In the Circle* (1969) for four electric guitars, bass, and percussion; *The Confessional Stone* (1969) for soprano and ten instruments (texts by Owen Dodson); *The Last Judgment* (1970) for women's chorus, narrator, piano, and percussion; and *Occurrences for Six.*

No discussion of the use of Afro-American folk material as a source of inspiration for art music would be complete without mention of the pioneering arrangements for voice and piano by Harry T. Burleigh (1866–1949). The first of these was "Deep River," published in 1916.

This was followed by two volumes of spirituals published by G. Ricordi & Co. Of them, *Musical America* (October 17, 1917) wrote: "They are one and all little masterpieces, settings by one of our time's most gifted song composers of melodies, which he penetrates as probably no other living composer."

Burleigh himself wrote on October 25, 1924, in the *New York World*: "My desire was to preserve them in harmonies that belong to modern methods of tonal progression without robbing the melodies of their racial flavor." These settings have been used by great concert artists everywhere.

12   Primous Fountain and the Amaks

"Place our work on programs with Beethoven, Mozart, Schoenberg, Copland, and the current avant-gardists. We don't even have to be called Black. When we stand for our bows, that fact will become clear when it should: *After the work has made its own impact.*"

This frequently quoted statement by Hale Smith represents a point of view held by many of our Black composers of concert music. Whether or not he subscribes to Smith's view, this is the position in which Primous Fountain III (b. 1949) found himself on Sunday afternoon, February 20, 1977, at Carnegie Hall.

When his *Ritual Dances of the Amaks* received its New York premiere by the Buffalo Philharmonic under the direction of Michael Tilson Thomas, it shared the program with Brahms' *Tragic* Overture in D minor (Opus 81) and Rachmaninoff's Piano Concerto No. 3 in D minor (Opus 30.)

Fountain first came to national attention when he won the Young Composers Award of Broadcast Music, Inc. In 1974, he also became the youngest person ever to receive a Guggenheim Fellowship.

Ritual Dances of the Amaks is the result of a 1972 commission by the Fromm Foundation and received its first performance at the Festival of Contemporary Music at Tanglewood under Gunther Schuller. It has also been played by the Minnesota Orchestra in 1975.

According to the program notes, the Amaks were a proud

and ancient people and great warriors, feared because of the mysterious powers they possessed. The composer has given us one hint toward his approach to his subject matter when he called it "mythic-satirical in nature."

The element of satire seemed missing in Sunday's performance by the orchestra. It was somewhat reminiscent of Stravinsky's *The Rites of Spring*, with some striking sonorities in the brass. The use of percussion, particularly in the last of its three movements, seemed very tame indeed.

In spite of these reservations, Fountain impresses me as a young composer who bears watching. He has already acquired considerable skill in orchestration, and his effects are never achieved in a less than very musical manner. For now, this is as much as one has a right to expect.[11]

Primous Fountain (b. 1949) began composing music at the age of fifteen. His ballet *Manifestation* has been choreographed by Arthur Mitchell for the Dance Theatre of Harlem. He has also completed a cello concerto on commission for the Minnesota Orchestra. His music has been performed by the Chicago Symphony, the Oakland Symphony, the Buffalo Philharmonic, and by an orchestra conducted by Gunther Schuller at the Festival of Contemporary Music at Tanglewood.

13   Black Brazilian Composers

Dr. Robert Pritchard epiphanized at the United Nations on Thursday, May 20, 1976, to preside over a three-hour musical celebration of the thirteenth anniversary of the Organization of African Unity. It has taken me this long (until June 12, 1976) to recover sufficiently to commit my impressions to newsprint.

What drew me to the concert was the fact that works by three rarely performed Brazilian Mulatto composers would be heard. These were José Joachim Lobo de Mesquita (born c. 1805), Ignacio Perreira Neves (1730–c.1792), and José Mauricio Nuñes Garcia (1767–1830).

Mesquita and Neves, both from the Minas Gerais area, were represented by a Mass in Fa and a *Credo*, respectively. A *Laudate Pueri* by Garcia of Rio de Janeiro added dimension to the geography. The latter composer is represented on the Columbia Records Black Composers Series, Volume 5.

As expected, the works sounded like Haydn and other European composers of the period, which is not bad. But religious music, when taken from its natural habitat, the church, is not my idea of an evening's entertainment in the concert hall.

Under the skillful direction of Kermit Moore, the Festival of the New World Symphony played well, assisted by the excellent glee clubs of Spelman and Morehouse Colleges. The distinguished soloists included Olga Iglesias (Puerto Rico), Paulette St. Lot (Haiti), George Shirley (U.S.A.), and Rawn Spearman (U.S.A.).[12]

By far the most important of these Black Brazilian composers was José Mauricio Nuñes Garcia. The *Catalogo tematico das obras do Padre José Mauricio Nuñes Garcia* by Cleofe Person de Mattos (Rio de Janeiro, 1970) shows that his total output amounted to some 419 works.

Born in Rio de Janeiro, Garcia devoted most of his attention to religious music. However, he also wrote an opera *Le Due Gemele,* some songs, twelve divertimentos, a string quartet, a piano solo, three secular works for chorus and orchestra, and four works for orchestra.

Columbia's Black Composers Series has devoted a complete disk to his Requiem Mass with the Helsinki Philharmonic under Paul Freeman. The Morgan State College Choir is featured, with soloists Doralene Davis (soprano), Betty Allen (mezzo), William Brown (tenor), and Matti Tuloisela (bass-baritone).

14 Black Women in Music

Musical scholars, critics, and students from around the country gathered at Atlanta University Center for its fifth annual Workshop on Afro-American Music, January 29 through 31, 1976. With Clark College as host institution, the coordinators were Dr. Florence Robinson, Harriette W. Bell, and Dr. Richard A. Long.

The opening session was conducted by Dr. Robinson, with Dr. Frederick Hall, Sr., of Dillard University presiding. It was entitled "The Role of Black Women in Music." In the afternoon, I delivered a lecture on the outstanding composer Margaret Bonds (1913–1972), with Dr. Robinson standing in for Dr. Roland Allison of Clark, who was to have presided.

In respect to Dr. Vivian Henderson, president of Clark College, who had just died, an informal concert of music by Black women composers was cancelled. Because the students of the various music departments of the university invested so much time in its preparation, I certainly hope that the event will be rescheduled some time in the future.

One of the most rewarding sessions took place when Dr. Johnson Hubert of Morris Brown College led a round table discussion of "Research in Progress." After Dr. Hubert gave an impressive account of his own research in African music, the participants spoke of their own projects and how they were disseminating information.

It was fascinating to hear Dr. Hall speak of his travels to Europe to disprove the racist theory propagated by George Pullen Jackson that Black spirituals were imitations of their white counterparts. This led to a lively dialogue between him and Dr. Orrin Clayton Suthern II (Lincoln University). They shared with us valuable information on the special character-istics of the Black singing voice.[13]

The fifth annual Workshop on Afro-American Music de-voted to "The Role of Black Women in Music" at the Atlanta University Center is of more than passing interest. It focused attention on the careers of four Black women composers who have made notable contributions to the American musical scene.

Florence Price (1888–1953), a native of Little Rock, Ar-kansas, became the first Black woman in the United States to win recognition as a composer. A graduate of the New Eng-land Conservatory of Music, where she studied with Chad-wick and Converse, she continued her studies in Chicago.

According to the 1966 *ASCAP Biographical Dictionary*, her musical output covered a wide range. She wrote symphonies, concertos, chamber works, art songs, solo pieces for piano and violin, and settings for voice and piano of Black American spirituals.

Today Miss Price is remembered solely for her arrangement of "My Soul's Been Anchored in the Lord." Almost every Black concert singer has at some time programmed this piece, and it has become a classic. In spite of a rather operatic ending, it captures the spirit of genuine Black folk style.

During the Century of Progress World's Fair, Dr. Frederick Stock introduced her Symphony in E Minor. The *Chicago Daily News* reported: "It is a faultless work, a work that speaks its own message with restraint and yet with passion . . . worthy of a place in the regular symphonic repertory."

Miss Marian Anderson introduced Miss Price's "Songs to the Dark Virgin." *Chicago Daily News* critic Eugene Stinson wrote that it had "one of the greatest immediate successes ever won by an American song." Unfortunately, this song has completely disappeared from the repertory of singers.

In 1934, the pianist Margaret Bonds played Miss Price's Concerto in F Minor with the Women's Symphony in Chicago. The *Chicago Herald and Examiner* reported: "It is full of fine melodies . . . the piano part was expertly set upon the keyboard and was brilliantly played by Margaret Bonds."

Inspired by the success of her friend and colleague, Florence Price, Margaret Bonds (1913–1972) early turned her attention to composition. She earned a master's degree from Northwestern University and later studied at Juilliard. Her awards and fellowships included a Rosenwald, Roy Harris, and Wanamaker.

One of Miss Bonds' earliest works to attract attention was a setting of Langston Hughes' classic poem "The Negro Speaks of Rivers." Published by Handy Brothers and now out of print, this song has been in the repertory of such singers as Etta Moten, Rawn Spearman, and Lawrence Winters.

Later, Miss Bonds became a personal friend of the poet, and they collaborated on one of her most popular works, a cantata for solo voices, chorus, and orchestra entitled *The Ballad of the Brown King*. It is performed annually in many Black churches throughout the country.

While preparing my lecture on Miss Bonds for Atlanta, I found a privately made recording of Rawn Spearman singing her cycle *Three Dream Portraits* (words by Langston Hughes). Repeated hearings and close study of the score lead me to believe that this is her finest piece of writing for voice and piano.

In the catalogue of Mercury Music Corporation are a number of her settings of spirituals for concert use. Many of these have been widely performed by Leontyne Price, who also included several (orchestrated by the composer) in the RCA album *Swing Low, Sweet Chariot*.

Less known, but most interesting are two instrumental pieces based on the spiritual "Wade in the Water," both titled "Troubled Water." One is an eight-minute cello version dedicated to Kermit Moore (August 3, 1964), and the other is a piano setting frequently played by Frances Walker.

Of the former, Moore wrote: "Although this was Margaret Bonds' first attempt to write for the cello, the piece is very skillfully written. It is extremely difficult for both cellist and pianist and requires performers of great ability." The manuscript is in the private library of Moore.

Among her larger works is a Mass in D Minor for chorus and orchestra, background music for *Shakespeare in Harlem* (adapted from Langston Hughes' works by Robert Glenn) and incidental music for *U.S.A.* (adapted from works by John Dos Passos). The mass has not been performed as yet.

One is impressed with the high degree of musicality and fine craftsmanship in her works. Her musical ideas are not particularly original. But, as she says in her unpublished *A*

Reminiscence (1967), "I came to realize that most composers at one time or another reflect their friends."

Julia Perry (b. 1927) first came to my attention when her *Stabat Mater* for contralto and orchestra was featured by Newell Jenkins on a Clarion Concert in 1958. It was immediately clear that here was a composer of great individuality, daring, and technical skill.

On that occasion, her *Stabat Mater* was paired with one by Vivaldi, and it did not suffer by comparison. This was due to a magnificent performance by the orchestra and soloist Betty Allen. At the work's conclusion, the audience voiced its approval by a long ovation.

In his review in the *New York Times*, Ross Parmenter wrote: "The intensity of her feeling, frequently conveyed through vividly expressive string coloration, makes her work impressive, even though at times it seems to be somewhat lacking in form . . . she knows how to write effective declamation for the voice."

Born in Lexington, Kentucky, Miss Perry received her early training at Westminster Choir College and at Juilliard. She later worked with Luigi Dallapiccola and Nadia Boulanger. Among her many awards have been Guggenheim, American Academy, and National Institute of Arts and Letters fellowships.

Her *Study for Orchestra* was performed by the New York Philharmonic in 1965. Originally composed in Florence in 1952 and premiered by the Turin Symphony under Dean Dixon, it was revised twice. The first revision was played by the Little Orchestra Society under Thomas Sherman in 1955.

Of the Philharmonic performance, Harold Schoenberg (the *New York Times*) said: "[it] starts out in a buoyant manner and then bogs down, never fulfilling the promise of its initial statement. The harmonic idiom is neutral-modern but not too modern, lacking punch and personality."

On CRI Recordings (SD 252), one can hear her *Homunculus, C.F.* for ten percussionists with the Manhattan Percussion Ensemble. Composed in 1960, it was inspired by the experiment made by Faust's apprentice, Wagner, in which he brought to life a creature called homunculus.

Miss Perry has written two operas to date, *The Bottle* and *The Cask of Amontillado.* The latter was given its first performance here in 1954 at Columbia University. Her Requiem for Orchestra was performed as part of the Music in the Making series in 1959 at Cooper Union.

Retrospective concerts provide the listener with a chance to view a full-dimensional portrait of a composer. One can study in detail his or her musical character lines. "An Evening of Music by Dorothy Rudd Moore" on February 23, 1975, at Carnegie Recital Hall was such an occasion.

Like her physical countenance, her musical counterpart is one of extraordinary beauty. Peter G. Davis (the *New York Times*) observed: "The most arresting feature of Miss Moore's music is an original and often intense lyricism that pervades even the most complex harmonic and contrapuntal textures."

He went on to say: "Occasionally one feels that the musical ideas have not been developed as far as they might have been, but the expressive content of each piece shows a gifted and individual creative mind at work." I would say that this is a fair assessment of Miss Moore's work.

Covering a period of twelve years, the program included: Modes for String Quartet; Twelve Quatrains from *The Rubaiyat*; Dream and Variations for Piano Solo; Three Pieces for Violin and Piano; three songs from *The Dark Tower* and *The Weary Blues*; and *Dirge and Deliverance* for Cello and Piano.

A young woman, Miss Moore was graduated in 1963 from Howard University in Washington, D.C., where she studied with Mark Fax. She continued her studies with Nadia Boulanger and Chou Wen Chung. She has taught at New York University and the Bronx Community College.

After observing the musical activities of Miss Moore over a number of years, it is my feeling that she excels in the realm of vocal music. Her cycle *From the Dark Tower*, in version for mezzo soprano and orchestra, met with great success when it was performed in 1972 by Hilda Harris and the Symphony of the New World at Avery Fisher Hall. This belief was further strengthened when I heard the outstanding soprano Miriam Burton sing the premiere of a cycle *Sonnets on Love, Rosebuds and Death* in May of 1976 in Alice Tully Hall. At the time, I predicted that these songs would find their way onto many programs in the future.

15   Spotlight on Black Composers

The highlight of the 1964 annual convention of the National Association of Negro Musicians, held at Long Island University, was a program of symphonic music by Negro composers played by the Orchestra of America on Sunday evening August 16 in Philharmonic Hall. A near capacity audience gave generous applause to conductor Leonard DePaur and soloists Selwart Clarke, violist, and Billy Strayhorn, pianist.

Four works comprised the program: Negro Folk Symphony by William Dawson; Concerto no. 1 for Viola by Coleridge Taylor-Perkinson (world premiere); *Umbrian Scene* by Ulysses Kay; and "Night Creature" from *Symphonic Ellington* by Duke Ellington with an orchestration by Luther Henderson.

It would be unfair to judge the music too severely on this occasion, because the enormous expense involved in presenting such a program made adequate rehearsal time impossible. I found the Perkinson piece by far the most interesting. Written when the composer was twenty-one (1953), it is filled with original musical ideas, has a youthful freshness, and, in the slow movement, reveals genuine sensitivity.

Completed in 1932, the Dawson symphony was heard this time in a revised version. It seems overblown and empty, and I find it hard to believe that Leopold Stokowski has recently recorded it for Decca. Kay's *Umbrian Scene* is a fine piece of craftsmanship, while the Ellington work proved an unfortunate choice.

Special presentations were made to Duke Ellington and to Actors Equity for outstanding contributions to Negro musicians and actors, respectively. This concert was a benefit for the Scholarship Fund of the National Association of Negro Musicians. Congratulations are certainly in order to the many devoted people, both visible and invisible, who made it materialize.[14]

William Levi Dawson (b. 1898), a native of Anniston, Alabama, is best known for his work as director of the Tuskegee Institute Choir and for his unusually fine choral arrangements of Black American folk music. His Negro Folk Symphony was premiered in 1934 by Leopold Stokowski and the Philadelphia Orchestra. A critic of the *New York Times* observed that it had "dramatic feeling, a racial sensuousness and directness of melodic speech, and a barbaric turbulence." After a trip to West Africa in 1952, Dawson revised the work and it was recorded by the American Symphony Orchestra under Stokowski.

Coleridge-Taylor Perkinson (b. 1932), a native New Yorker, holds a bachelor's and a master's degree in composition from the Manhattan School of Music. He also studied at the Mozarteum in Salzburg and at the Berkshire Music Center. His Concerto for Viola and Orchestra (1954) was premiered by the Symphony of the New World. In 1964, he was commissioned by the Ford Foundation to write *Attitudes* for Metropolitan opera tenor George Shirley. It was premiered at the Metropolitan Museum of Art.

The National Association of Negro Musicians, which sponsored the Philharmonic Hall concert, was founded in 1919 by a group of distinguished Black musicians for the purpose of "stimulating progress, to discover and foster talent, to mold taste, to promote fellowship and to advocate racial expression."

It has branches in major cities throughout the country which promote its principles at a local level. But it is the annual convention which brings its members together with outstanding artists for workshops, seminars, and concerts on the highest artistic level.

16 Kansas City and the Jazz Heritage

Since Kansas City played such an important part in the history of jazz, it was fitting that the Kansas City Philharmonic should devote an entire program to that area of musical art on Tuesday evening, January 25, 1977, at Carnegie Hall. It was assisted by the Modern Jazz Quartet.

All of the works offered spanned the lifetime of Edward Kennedy (Duke) Ellington (1899–1974). There were jazz-influenced pieces by Debussy and Stravinsky and originals by Scott Joplin, Ellington, and John Lewis. The Modern Jazz Quartet also played a group of its specialties.

Two of the opening pieces were performed in transcriptions, having been written for piano solo. "Golliwog's Cake Walk" (Debussy, 1908) was orchestrated by Andre Caplet, and "Maple Leaf Rag" (Joplin, 1899) was transcribed anonymously in the famous *The Red Back Book* collection.

Stravinsky's "Ragtime" from *L'Histoire du Soldat* (1918) was heard in its original form. It is interesting to note that, at the time of its composition, the composer had only seen ragtime on published sheet music and never heard it played in performance.

This was followed by the Maurice Peress 1969 symphonic orchestration of the 1945 version of Ellington's classic suite *Black, Brown and Beige*. The original was first heard at Carnegie Hall on January 23, 1943, and was one of the composer's earliest efforts at working within a larger format.

Although Peress handled his task with considerable skill and taste, the end result robbed the work of its vitality and made it sound very square. He was not helped by the fact that his American-trained symphonic musicians were not equipped to deal with jazz performing style.

John Lewis's *In Memorium* for Jazz Quartet and Orchestra, heard in its New York premiere, came off more successfully. Here, the composer created a work that took into account the special tonal characteristics of a symphonic ensemble in combination with the Modern Jazz Quartet.[15]

✽   ✽   ✽

Duke Ellington made a number of excursions into the realm of the larger musical forms. Besides *Black, Brown and Beige* (1945), there is *A Drum Is a Woman* (1956), *Shakespearean* Suite (1957), *Nutcracker* Suite (1960), *Peer Gynt* Suite (1962), the two *Sacred Concerts, The River* (ballet, 1970), and an opera. Since most of Ellington's works were written with the special characteristics of his own orchestra in mind, it is next to impossible to adapt them to the symphonic ensemble.

17   Recordings: Black Piano Music

With her recording entitled *Natalie Hinderas Plays Music by Black Composers*, this remarkable artist opens up a treasure chest of piano works previously known only to the Black musical elite. It has been produced with loving care, annotated, and handsomely packaged by Desto (DC-7102/3).

Since her impressive New York debut at Town Hall in 1954, she has been slowly building a career as a major concert pianist. Besides giving recitals throughout the world, she has been soloist with the Cleveland Orchestra, the Philadelphia Orchestra, and the New York Philharmonic.

The composers represented on this recording are R. Nathaniel Dett (1882–1943), Thomas H. Kerr, Jr. (no date available), William Grant Still (b. 1895), John W. Work (1901–1968), George Walker (b. 1922), Arthur Cunningham (b. 1928), Stephen A. Chambers (b. 1940), Hale Smith (b. 1925), and Olly Wilson (b. 1937).

Dett's characteristic suite *In the Bottoms,* which consists of five moods and scenes reflecting Black life in the South, could sound banal in less skilled hands than Miss Hinderas's. Even the familiar "Juba Dance," brilliantly played here, is heard from a new perspective.

An absolutely charming little scherzino by Thomas Kerr, "Easter Monday Swagger," shows what the inspiration of a spiritual can produce in the hands of a fine composer. William Grant Still's "Three Visions" are as dazzling as newly cut diamonds, pieces which should be staples in the repertory.

John W. Work's suite *Scuppernong* is a marvelous evocation of the folk spirit. George Walker's Piano Sonata no. 1 (1953) is the first of a series of sonatas that are showing up on the programs of Black concert artists with growing frequency. Arthur Cunningham's *Engrams* shows great skill.

Stephen A. Chambers' (Talib Hakim) "Sound Gone," which utilizes a prepared piano, is not only inventive, but musical. Hale Smith's "Evocation" has rhythmic affinities with jazz phrasing although basically atonal. Olly Wilson's "Piano Piece" for piano and electronic sound is fascinating.

In less skilled hands, much of this material could fall flat. But Miss Hinderas has had the opportunity to play it on numerous tours to sharpen her perceptions. She has the skill of a virtuoso combined with extraordinary musicianship. She is, in short, a great artist.

R. Nathaniel Dett (1882–1943) was one of the first Black American composers to explore the area of piano suites. His complete piano works are again available by popular demand. He is also known for his choral arrangements of Afro-American spirituals and his oratorio *The Ordering of Moses*.

Thomas H. Kerr, Jr., holds three degrees from the Eastman School of Music. He has received a Rosenwald Fellowship (1942) and in 1944 received a prize in a contest sponsored by

Composers and Authors of America. A native of Baltimore, he has long been head of the Piano Department at Howard University.

John W. Work (1901–1968) was educated at Fisk, Columbia, and Yale universities, as well as at Juilliard. He has received a Rosenwald Fellowship. Long a member of the faculty of Fisk, his compositions include songs, choral pieces, and several orchestral works, including *Yenvalou*.

Arthur Cunningham (b. 1928) has studied at Columbia, Fisk, Juilliard, and Metropolitan Music School. He has written over four hundred songs in ballad-jazz-rock style, nearly one hundred piano pieces in various styles, and art songs, chamber works, and works for jazz and symphonic orchestras.

Talib Hakim (a.k.a. Stephen A. Chambers) was born in 1940 in Asheville, N.C. He was educated at the Manhattan School of Music, New York College of Music, and the New School. He has won the Bennington Composers' Conference Fellowship and ASCAP Composers Award. His orchestral works have been performed widely.

(The other composers on this recording have been covered elsewhere in this book.)

18   Rising Pride in Black Music

I have been impressed with several events that reflect the rising pride in Black achievement in the area of classical music. These include a revival of Scott Joplin's opera *Tree-monisha* on Friday, March 19, 1976 in Cleveland and *A Piano Festival* on February 29 in New York City.

A very enterprising young Cleveland conductor, Joseph R. Lynn, Jr., became happily obsessed by the idea of offering music by Scott Joplin to Cuyahoga Community College audiences under the auspices of the Department of Black Affairs. Despite many complications, he managed to bring the idea off nobly.

The program opened with a group of piano and vocal selections tied together with a narration. Pianist Clifford Jackson, an Oberlin student, gave brilliant readings of "Maple Leaf Rag," "Ragtime Dance" from a book of rag exercises by Joplin, and "Blink's Waltz."

Two young singers, Colenton Freeman and Gertrude Wilson, joined him in absolutely charming performances of the songs "Picture of Your Face" and "Pineapple Rag." It is to be hoped that more artists will dip into the treasure chest of Joplin goodies and offer a complete program of these songs.

But, the highlight of the program was a semi-staged version of *Treemonisha* with piano accompaniment. Conductor Lynn used a combination of youthful singers from the Cleveland area and members of the New York company, including soprano Kathleen Battle and choreographer Louis Johnson and four of his dancers.

Ms. Battle dominated the vocal proceedings in the title role. Her lovely, perfectly schooled voice was especially thrilling in the finale, "A Real Slow Drag." Jamelia Shahid (Monisha), Dennis Gillom (Ned), Colenton Freeman (Remus), and Willie Nichols (Parson Alltalk) revealed uncommon talent.

Choreographer Johnson helped smooth out the rough spots with great imagination and made this performance a meaningful experience for the young Clevelanders and their audience. The ballet sequences were handled with expertise and the Metro Liberation Chorale did themselves proud in the choral sections.

A *Piano Festival* was an outstanding event in our own Harlem community. It featured pianists Raymond Jackson, Frances Walker, and Robert Jordan in music by Black composers, many of whom once lived in Harlem.

The level of performance of this wonderful music was so high that it would be unfair to cite individual contributions by either the composers or the performers. I think that the standing ovation from the audience was an accurate and sufficient testimony to the quality of this truly festive occasion.

The composers represented were Samuel Coleridge-Taylor, Melville Charlton, Hall Johnson, Noel DaCosta, Coleridge-Taylor Perkinson, George Walker, Hale Smith, Howard Swanson, Margaret Bonds, Scott Joplin, Talib Rasul Hakim (Stephen Chambers), William Foster McDaniel, and R. Nathaniel Dett.[16]

Since this program is of special interest, I should like to list the works performed. They are: "Wade in the Water" and "Motherless Child" by Samuel Coleridge-Taylor (1875–1912); "Poeme Erotique" by Melville Charlton (1883–1973); "Polonaise" from *Chopin in Harlem* by Hall Johnson (1888–1970); "Clave Tune" and "Blue Tune" by Noel Da Costa (b. 1930); Toccata by Coleridge-Taylor Perkinson (b. 1932); Prelude and Caprice by George Walker (b. 1922); "Two Waltzes" by Samuel Coleridge-Taylor; "Faces of Jazz" by Hale Smith (b. 1925); "The Cuckoo" by Howard Swanson (b. 1907); "Troubled Waters" by Margaret Bonds (1913–1972); "Cascades" by Scott Joplin (1866–1917); Sonata no. 2 by George Walker; "Sound Gone" by Talib Rasul Hakim (Stephen Chambers, b. 1940); Toccata by William Foster McDaniel

(b. 1940); and "Juba Dance" from *In The Bottoms* by R. Nathaniel Dett (1882–1943).

I am offering a biography only of William Foster McDaniel, who does not appear elsewhere in this volume. A pianist and composer, he is a native of Columbus, Ohio. He has a B.M. degree from Capital University and an M.A. from Boston University. He has been a Fulbright Scholar in Paris and a first-prize winner in a piano competition by the National Association of Negro Musicians. His Concerto for Piano and Orchestra (1975) has been performed by the New Symphony in New York and the Yonkers Civic Philharmonic. He has also composed a Sonata for Piano, a Woodwind Quintet, and *Five Songs with Debra* for voice and piano.

For those who are interested in further exploration of Black piano music, I would like to suggest a doctoral dissertation, "The Piano Music of Twentieth Century Black Americans as Illustrated Mainly in the Works of Three Composers" by Raymond Jackson (1973). It is now on file at the Juilliard School in New York City. Besides containing an analysis of three major works by R. Nathaniel Dett, Howard Swanson, and George Walker, it has an excellent introduction to the entire repertory.

19   New Music by Black Composers

During the intermission of a program of new music by Black composers on Sunday, February 27, 1977 at the Billie Holiday Theatre in Brooklyn, a lady came up to me and said:

"I can't wait to read your review in the *Amsterdam News* to find out what I should think about this music."

At first I was flattered to think that my opinion of a musical event meant that much to someone. Then I became so curious about *her* reactions that I invited her to share them with me after the concert. They were provocative and provide insight into the way some people listen to music.

She found Hale Smith's Introduction, Cadenzas and Interludes for Eight Players "like an exhibition of beautifully moulded sound sculptures." Julius Eastman's Conceptual Music for the Piano "reminded me of Little Schroeder of 'Peanuts' in brownface trying to play modern music."

Dorothy Rudd Moore's Trio Number One for Piano, Violin and Cello was "classic in structure and had lots of feeling." Omar Clay's Three Short Pieces for Flute had "charm, like *haiku*." His *Chun Dynasty* for Marimba and Violin was "like a Chinese ritual."

Noel Da Costa's *Occurrences for Six* was "pure Jackson Pollack translated into sound." Carman Moore's *Museum Piece* for Flute, Cello and Tape was a "collage made up of scraps from here and there." Oliver Lake's Piece for Three Violins and Improvisor was "brilliant jazz improvisation."

I doubt if anyone in the large audience had a dull moment all afternoon. Coordinated by Tania Leon and Talib Hakim, the program included music representing a wide variety of composing styles. And, all of it was played by an ensemble of an exceptionally high caliber.

The concert was part of a new series of community concerts under the auspices of the Brooklyn Philharmonic. Its aim is to provide a forum for Black composers and to encourage Black participation in the orchestra's activities. This is a project which deserves your support.[17]

❖   ❖   ❖

Except for those who appear elsewhere in this book, here are biographies of the composers, as taken from the program notes:

Omar Clay, composer and percussionist, has long been associated with the Brooklyn Philharmonia. He has taught music in the New York City public schools and throughout the United States and Europe, and is on the staff of the Third Street Music School. He has recorded and performed with singing stars Dionne Warwick and Sarah Vaughan, and his noted percussion ensemble M'Boom includes musicians Warren Smith, Max Roach, Roy Brooks, Freddie Waits, and Joe Chambers.

Julius Eastman studied piano and composition at the Curtis Institute in Philadelphia. He has worked with Buffalo's Center for the Creative and Performing Arts and was a member of the faculty of that city's university for six years. To his compositional and pianistic talents can be added a firm reputation as a singer of the music of such contemporary artists as Peter Maxwell Davies and Hans Werner Henze.

Oliver Lake, a current recipient of the Creatives Artists Public Service Program's Fellowship, writes music rooted in the Black musical tradition for his quartet as well as string music for trio and works for jazz orchestra. He also plays alto sax and flute. A section from his album *Heavy Spirits* is being used in the Broadway play *For Colored Girls Who Have Considered Suicide When the Rainbow Is Enuf*.

Many of the people connected with this project were part of the Society of Black Composers, which was organized in 1968 with the purpose "to provide a permanent forum for the works and thoughts of Black composers, to collect and disseminate information about Black composers and their activities, and to enrich the cultural life of the community at large." With the assistance of a grant from Columbia University, the society presented a number of major concerts in the New York area.

Indispensable to anyone interested in music by Black people is the Black Composers Series of recordings prepared in collaboration with the Afro-American Music Opportunities Association (AAMOA) and Music for Educational and Cultural Appreciation (MECA) and produced by Columbia Masterworks. The first four volumes, which were issued in 1974, were received with much critical acclaim.

The artistic director for this series is Dr. Paul Freeman, who is conductor-in-residence with the Detroit Symphony Orchestra. Dr. Dominque-Rene De Lerma is chief consultant. Research for this project was conducted under a grant from the National Endowment for the Arts.

I should also like to recommend an unusually fine periodical. *The Black Perspective in Music*, edited with great care by Dr. Eileen Southern. It is published by the Foundation for Research in the Afro-American Creative Arts, Inc., P.O. Drawer 1, Cambria Heights, New York 11411.

II

SINGERS

20   The Art of Roland Hayes

Several years ago, I remember asking the celebrated Metropolitan Opera Singer Alexander Kipnis if there was any American who really knew how to sing German Lieder in the tradition of native exponents. He thought carefully and replied: "In Berlin I once heard a Roland Hayes. If he is still alive. . . ."

Mr. Hayes was still very much alive. At that time, aged seventy-eight, he was touring colleges and music schools, giving seminars in song interpretation. Also he continued to teach his regular students in his lovely home in Brookline, Massachusetts. On very rare occasions, he would give a recital.

Mr. Hayes was the first Black singer to be accepted on the major concert stages of the United States. When he went to the management of Symphony Hall in Boston in 1917 to engage it for his local debut, the person in charge froze in shock at the prospect of a Black gracing that hallowed stage.

It is now history that Mr. Hayes eventually became internationally acclaimed as a singer of art songs. The *Boston Post* called him "the greatest recitalist in the world." The critic of the *Copenhagen Politiken* stated: "The fascinating thing in his art of singing is the intensity by which he lives through every song."

For those who were not fortunate enough to hear the seminars given by Mr. Hayes, there is a two-record album entitled *The Art of Roland Hayes* (*Six Centuries of Song*) on Vanguard (VRS-448-9), which preserves for posterity the singing of one of the world's greatest artists. It belongs in the library of every serious collector.

The songs range from Guillaume de Machaut (c. 1300–1377) to Claude Debussy (1862–1918). They are sung in the original French, German, Italian, and Russian with exemplary diction. Then, of course, there are a number of Afro-American religious folksongs offered in unusually fine settings arranged by Mr. Hayes himself.

In his later years, time had taken its toll on his instrument, and there was evidence of strain in the upper register, But, the middle and low tones remained as lovely as ever. More important was the fact that Mr. Hayes had that rare ability to take a text and make it appear as if it came directly out of his own experience. He showed the listener what Lieder singing is all about.[1]

Saturday night, December 1, 1923, the night Roland Hayes first sang in Town Hall, marks a dividing line in the history of Blacks in classical music. Before that date an occasional performer a Black Patti or a Blind Tom, achieved some fame, but none had found a secure place in the mainstream of classical music. Whatever their talent, they usually performed in vaudeville, not in the concert hall. After that night Black performers, particularly Black singers, became a regular part of the concert scene. Five months later Marian Anderson sang her initial Town Hall recital and Jules Bledsoe made his debut in Aeolian Hall, and a year after that Paul Robeson sang his famous first concert of spirituals.

It would be hard to overestimate the impact Roland Hayes made that night at Town Hall and impossible to compare it with any musical event of more recent years. He was, in the true sense of an overused word, a sensation. "He astounds and delights," the *New York Times* critic wrote, "by virtue of both natural and cultivated beauty of voice." The public demanded to hear him. A second Town Hall recital followed only a month after the first. This time there were seats on the stage. But even that was not enough. Another month later we find in the *Times*: "The third and farewell appearance of Roland Hayes, the remarkable negro artist, drew to Carnegie Hall in yesterday's storm an audience that packed even the stage and thronged the footlights for encores . . . Roland Hayes' beautiful natural voice, native emotional power, developed artistry and pure enunciation of foreign texts again enthralled hearers, white and black."

New York's sudden though belated discovery of Roland Hayes (he was thirty-six years old) came when he was already a celebrity in Europe and had sung all over the United States—including New York. Indeed, two years earlier, the black critic and composer, Penman Lovingood in his *Famous Modern Negro Musicians* (New York: 1921) had acclaimed Hayes as "the foremost recitalist of his race" and observed that he owed this position to the "power of persistence, of faith and vision."

Roland Hayes certainly needed those qualities as he traveled the long road from a poverty-stricken tenant farm in Georgia, where he was born in 1887, to the pinnacle of the concert world. Both his parents had once been slaves. His father died when Roland was twelve. His mother, a remarkable woman he later called "Angel Mo," struggled to support her children and even aspired to an education for them. As a teenager Roland worked in an iron foundry in Chattanooga. At the home of a white man for whom he sang, he was introduced to phonograph records by Caruso and Sembrich. That night, Hayes said later, "I was born again. It was as if a bell had been struck that rang in my heart. And it has never ceased to ring there."

There were many jobs along the way, farm-hand, laborer, waiter, butler, messenger, but his goal was set. He managed to attend the preparatory department of Fisk University, where he sang for a time with the Fisk Jubilee Singers. While on tour with that group to Boston in 1911, he decided to remain there. He was able to arrange for voice lessons with a distinguished teacher, Arthur Hubbard. He brought his mother north to live with him. At first they struggled for the barest necessities, using boxes as beds and chairs. For decades after he became successful he lived in a large white frame house in Brookline, a Boston suburb. There he died on the last day of 1976 at the age of eighty-nine.

The first known recital by Roland Hayes took place at Steinert Hall, Boston, in 1912. Three years later with William Richardson, baritone, and William Lawrence, pianist, (who remained his accompanist for many years) he toured the United States, performing mainly in Negro churches as a member of the Hayes Trio. That same year he sang in Jordan Hall, Boston, and received favorable reviews. In 1917 he raised enough money to rent Boston's famous Symphony Hall and filled it, chiefly with fellow employees of the John Hancock Insurance Company who had heard him sing while at work.

His New York debut was at Aeolian Hall in 1917 and he sang there again on January 30, 1919, with Harry T. Burleigh at the piano. The *Times* review, headed "Roland Hayes in Plantation Songs," said: "He is one of those with natural voices who has not lost in cultivation that rare gift of unctuous humor and pathos of his race." Included in the program were songs by Burleigh and one by Coleridge-Taylor as well as "The Dream" from Massenet's *Manon.* A year later the *Times* of March 12, 1920, noted that Rowland (sic) W. Hayes had sung "primitive African airs" in Aeolian Hall the night before. The patronizing critic, ignoring the long years of careful preparation, preferred to view him as "one of those whose music is a natural gift that 'just grows' and whose voice has the clear, ringing appeal traditional with his race." No wonder that Hayes, in his authorized biography *Angel Mo' and Her Son Roland Hayes* (1942) does not mention these Aeolian Hall recitals.

No wonder also that he decided to try his luck in Europe. Like so many other American singers he found that the best way to build a career in America was to leave it. After several recitals in London, he gave a command performance for King George V and Queen Mary at Buckingham Palace on April 13, 1921. Acclaimed by English, French, and German critics as one of the great voices of the world, he returned to his own country, which was now waiting to welcome him. He sang with the Boston Symphony under Pierre Monteux on November 17, 1923—the first Black to sing with a major American orchestra—and that triumph was quickly followed by his conquest of New York.

All of America now clamored to hear him. One season he did 125 recitals. Each year in New York, he gave not one but two, three, four, or even more. For a decade he traveled almost continuously, European tours alternating with American tours. In addition to recitals, he also performed with many of the leading orchestras of the world. The sheer number of recitals dropped as the years went by, but the public response never wavered. During World War II he was flown by bomber to England where he sang to two audiences of ten thousand each in London's Albert Hall. As late as his seventy-fifth birthday recital on June 3, 1962, he was still able to fill Carnegie Hall. On that occasion Virgil Thomson, speaking for a host of celebrities, said: "You do us an honor to sing for us today and you do the human race an honor to exist." This was the last major New York recital by Roland Hayes.

In his later years Hayes was often perceived by Blacks as a somewhat special person living in the rarefied realm of Lieder, far removed from the problems and aspirations of his people. He certainly was not an activist as that term came to be defined in the sixties, yet he shared fully in the Black experience and his contributions were enormous and permanent, and he richly deserved the Spingarn Medal awarded him in 1924.

"I believed," he once said, "there was a place in this world for a Negro concert artist, and I proved it." In doing so, he opened the concert halls of the world to Black artists. He was the first Black to sing before mixed audiences in the South, and he sang to a non-segregated audience in Washington's Constitution Hall thirteen years before the D.A.R. refused that hall to Marian Anderson.

Nor did he escape the usual racial indignities along the way. In his youth he once sang in a club in Louisville—from behind a curtain so that no one would know he was black. Even in 1942, when he had long been world famous, he was arrested and beaten by the police in Rome, Georgia, when he went to rescue his wife who had sat in the white section of a shoe store.

His career, successful as it was, did not bring him some of the opportunities a white singer would have had. He never had the chance to sing opera. Olin Downes, writing in 1955 of the signing of Marian Anderson by the Met, recalled those Blacks who might have sung there, including Roland Hayes "in his youth, when a lyrical tenor part such as Don Ottavio or perhaps Des Grieux would not have been outside his vocal and dramatic range of effective interpretation."

Today, when Hayes is remembered chiefly as a Lieder singer, his lifelong devotion to spirituals is sometimes lost sight of. Harry Burleigh was probably the first to arrange them for solo voice instead of chorus, and Robeson achieved great fame for his singing of them, but it was Hayes who made them a standard part of a solo song recital and thus brought them to the attention of serious concertgoers. He also made a notable contribution in arranging spirituals, next only to Burleigh and Hall Johnson. To his collection of arrangements, he gave the title *My Songs* because, as he explains in the introduction, "The experience from which they have sprung have been so much a part of my life that the songs have become part of me. They speak to me clearly, echoing the dim past—our ancient African ancestry and tribal memories." His own great grandfather, who was brought from the Ivory Coast in 1790, was said to have sung "He Never Said a Mumblin' Word," which was frequently included in a Hayes recital. He believed that "the Negro has his God-given music to bring to the sum total of good in the world; his future lies in the recognition of his heritage, the preservation of the songs of his fathers."

At a significant moment in his life, he asked himself: "What did I know of myself, of my people? Here we are in America. We were lifted out of our old environment and set down here, aliens in body and soul. Shreds and tatters of our ancient qualities still cling to us even now, but what was the original fabric like?"

He always wanted to go to Africa to try to find out. He especially wanted, of course, to study the relationship of African music to what he termed Afro-American religious folk songs. Indeed, he first went to Europe in 1920 with the plan of going on to Africa, but he never got there and had to content himself with what he could learn from Africans he met in London and Paris. "That's how I got to know about my African roots," he said.

He came to realize very early in his career that "even the voice I was born with was colored." In 1918, he recalled, "I had not yet gotten over trying to sing like a white man. I began to listen more clearly to white singers and to my amazement I discovered that their voices were as white as their skins." The black critic, Penman Lovingood, noted that "The singular qualities of racial appeal have been meaningly (sic) kept his his voice" and that his success was "directly traceable to these qualities."

The Hayes voice was never a big one, but it was of surpassing beauty. "Tender and velvety and capable of the most delicate pianos," one critic wrote in 1924. The limitations were apparent even then. The same critic noted that "he showed some tendency to force his higher notes in the forte passages." But even twenty years later Olin Downes could write that his voice was "unforgettable for tonal beauty and poetic illusion . . . for sentiment that was never affected or exaggerated and a simplicity that few singers attain." Hayes's diction was always remarkable. Early critics found it surprising that a Negro could pronounce foreign texts so well (or perhaps at all); later on, his diction was appreciated as one element in his artistry.

It was the total effect that was stunning. As John Wolffers wrote in the *Boston Herald*: "Roland Hayes does not sing a song, he lives it. All his knowledge, all his talent, his artistry, is focused on one thing only—the meaning behind the words."

He sang with his entire body. The characteristic gesture was the raising of his clasped hands. Other times his left hand moved in front of him as if tracing out the words. His eyes were often closed, so complete was his absorption in the music. As *Pravda* noted "one forgets about the artist as interpreter who comes between the audience and the song."

A typical Hayes program ranged from Handel, Bach, and Purcell, through Haydn, Mozart, and Schubert to Berlioz and Debussy—and spirituals. Occasionally there was an operatic aria or a bow to contemporary composers. Lovingood notes "Hayes's untiring effort to make his programs interesting."

As Hayes grew older, his hair turned gray and then white, but the slender rather short figure remained eternally boyish. The voice, of course, changed and its limitations, particularly at the top, became more apparent. Upon the occasion of his seventy-fifth birthday recital in Carnegie Hall, Howard Klein, the *Times* critic, wrote:

Mr Hayes's singing at this stage of his 50 year career suggests the qualities of a fine old piano. The surface has been cracked by time, and the colors are less brilliant than when they were new. But beneath the exterior defects, the undiminished strength and power of the original are clearly outlined. His artistic projection was magnetic. His coiled-spring delivery accommodated itself to the different moods encompassing the light, floating Schubertian phrases and the impassioned simplicity of the spirituals.

There was a radiance in Roland Hayes—call it soul perhaps—which shone through almost everything he sang. A sensitive critic put this special quality in these words: "The white-haired figure on the platform embodied the aspirations, the innate goodness, the brotherhood of all mankind."

21   Miss Anderson's Farewell

During her farewell recital on Easter Sunday afternoon, April 18, 1965, at Carnegie Hall, contralto Marian Anderson sang a setting of Langston Hughes' poem "The Negro Speaks of Rivers." It describes the rivers associated with Negro history, ending with the line "My soul has grown deep, like the rivers."

Miss Anderson has known these rivers in a long career on the concert stage which has taken her around the world. Like the poet, she has experienced many trials and tribulations and not only survived, but triumphed over them. Her soul has truly grown deep like the rivers.

For this occasion, Miss Anderson chose songs which had long been associated with her career. Composers represented included Handel, Haydn, Schubert, Barber, Swanson, Britten and Quilter. She closed with her usual group of Afro-American religious folk songs.

Miss Anderson's voice was then only a thread of the magnificent instrument it had been. Occasionally, in such songs as Schubert's "Der Doppelgaenger," tones of considerable richness crept through. But her powers of communication had not dimmed and she held us spellbound.

When I first heard Miss Anderson sing Lieder, I felt that she approached them with too much timidity. Although she had worked out the musical and interpretive details with great care, she always seemed to keep a respectful distance between herself and the material.

This was no longer true, nor had it been for many years. Her art had so deepened with time that the singer and the song had become one. The message of the text seemed to come out of her own personal experience. This is, of course, what great recital singing is all about.

It was clear from her first entrance that Sunday afternoon that Miss Anderson wanted her farewell to be a joyous occasion. She greeted us with a warm, infectious smile somewhat like a hostess at a bon voyage party. And, we sent her off on her journey with a well-deserved standing ovation.[2]

In more than fifty years as a singer, Marian Anderson really had three separate careers. In the first, she sang within the Black community, mainly in churches. The second, in the mid-1920s, was successful but short-lived. The third, her greatest career, came relatively late and, like so many others, she had to go to Europe to be recognized. Had the opportunity to sing opera come sooner, she would have had yet a fourth career as an opera star.

Blacks discovered Marian Anderson long before whites. Born February 27, 1902, in Philadelphia, she began to sing at a very early age in the junior choir of the Union Baptist

Church. At the precocious age of eight, she graduated to the "grown-up" choir. She was soon singing professionally at recitals and concerts in Philadelphia and other cities. As early as 1921, when she was still in her teens, her fame had spread so widely in Black communities that the Black critic, Penman Lovingood, in his *Famous Modern Negro Musicians*, could write: "Miss Anderson possesses the most perfect vocal organ . . . in the race. She gives forth a prodigality of voice and tone that is unmatched in its wealth."

Her second career began auspiciously with a Town Hall recital on April 25, 1924, only a few months after Roland Hayes had captured the concert world. The *New York Times* reviewer wrote: "A song recital of a promising character was given by Marian Anderson . . . the singer had a mezzo of volume and strength." The next year, in a contest sponsored by the New York Philharmonic that attracted three hundred entrants, she won first prize, an appearance with the orchestra at Lewisohn Stadium. But then, as young singers frequently find, concert managers did not seem to notice. A career that had barely begun seemed ended.

From her early childhood, funds to provide for vocal study had been raised by those who had confidence in her. Now, the National Association of Negro Musicians awarded her a scholarship, and later the Julius Rosenwald Fund assisted her. She went to Europe to immerse herself in the cultures and languages of the peoples whose music she sang. There, in the early 1930s, she was "discovered." Beginning in 1933, her long European tours became triumphs. Toscanini, hearing her at Salzburg, declared, "A voice like yours is heard only once in a hundred years." Finally, Sol Hurok heard her in Paris and persuaded her to return to America. She came home already a celebrity.

Her Town Hall "debut" took place December 30, 1935—the one eleven years earlier is usually overlooked—and it marked the beginning of the greatest recital career of our time. Of her voice the *Times* said: "It is a contralto of stunning range and volume managed with suppleness and grace. It is a voice that lends itself to the entire emotional gamut, responsive to delicate nuance and able to swell out with opulence and sonority." So great was the public interest that a second recital took place in Carnegie Hall only a month later, and yet a third six weeks after that.

The whole country wanted to hear her. In 1938 she sang seventy recitals, one of the longest tours by a singer in concert history, but that was surpassed the next season when she sang ninety-two recitals in seventy cities, including five in Carnegie Hall. These long American tours, interspersed with repeated tours of Europe and South America, continued until her retirement. She sang also in Australia, the Soviet Union, Israel, and throughout much of Asia. Perhaps her largest audiences were for her regular appearances on radio's Telephone Hour. She also made many RCA Victor records of which, unfortunately, only two or three remain in the catalogue.

In 1939 the Daughters of the American Revolution denied Miss Anderson the use of Constitution Hall in Washington for a recital. A national furor resulted; Mrs. Franklin D. Roosevelt resigned from that organization in protest, and the United States government offered Miss Anderson the use of the Lincoln Memorial for an outdoor recital. On Easter Sunday, 1939, 75,000 Americans gathered in front of the Lincoln statue and stretched to the end of the lagoon to hear her sing. Behind her as she sang sat members of the Cabinet, the Supreme Court, and Congress. Radio carried the event throughout the land. A large mural in the Department of the Interior Building commemorates the event. (The D.A.R. invited Miss Anderson to sing in Constitution Hall in 1943.)

Honors were showered on Miss Anderson. As early as 1936 she was invited by President and Mrs. Roosevelt to sing at the White House, the first Negro to do so. In 1938 Howard University conferred upon her the first of the twenty-four Doctorates of Music she was to receive, and the NAACP awarded her the Spingarn Medal the same year. She received the Bok Award for 1941 and used the $10,000.00 proceeds to establish the Marian Anderson Award for young singers. Among the winners have been Camilla Williams, Mattiwilda Dobbs, and Grace Bumbry.

Marian Anderson had become much more than a performer. For the quarter century between her Lincoln Memorial recital and her retirement, she was a public personality, a national treasure, whose presence made an event "official." In 1939, on the eve of World War II, she sang at the White House for the visiting King George and Queen Elizabeth of Great Britain. During the war she toured military camps, hospitals, and war factories. Forty thousand air cadets paraded for her at Sheppard Field, Texas. She appeared with Stokowski and the Westminster Choir in a film shown in combat areas around the world on Christmas Day, 1944. When General De Gaulle visited America, she sang "La Marseillaise" for him at Lewisohn Stadium. She sang the "Star Spangled Banner" at New York's mammoth V-E Day reception for General Eisenhower. She was at Hyde Park for the dedication of the Roosevelt Memorial Library. She sang for the American troops in Korea. In 1957, under the sponsorship of the State Department, she made a long tour of India and the countries of southeast Asia and the Far East; she was received everywhere by heads of state and ordinary people not only as a supreme artist but as a representative of the best in America. The trip was filmed for Edward R. Murrow's "See It Now."

The next year President Eisenhower appointed her a member of the United States delegation to the United Nations. She was invited to sing at President Kennedy's inaugural. She sang for American forces in beleagured Berlin on Christmas Day 1961. The next March she sang in the new State Department auditorium in Washington for the President's Cabinet, the Congress, the Supreme Court, and the diplomatic corps.

With all her triumphs, one field of singing remained unconquered until very late in her career. At long last, on October 7, 1954, the Metropolitan Opera Association, rigidly closed to Black singers since its founding, announced that Marian Anderson would make her Met debut that season. Humbly overjoyed, she said: "Ever since one was in high school, one wanted to sing opera—at the Metropolitan if that could be."

The event took place January 7, 1955. The opera was Verdi's *Un Ballo in Maschera* in which she sang Ulrica, a short but pivotal role. "History was made last night," Olin Downes wrote in the *Times*.

Miss Anderson received a thunderous ovation. . . . She proceeded with her first aria, "Re dell'abisse". The passage suited well the dark and rich color of the voice as the simplicity and eloquence of Miss Anderson's singing graced the song. At first . . . she wavered a little in pitch. But before the aria was finished, the singer had demonstrated the same musicianship and instinct for dramatic communication that she has long demonstrated on the concert stage. In Ulrica's half-act, by her native sensibility, intelligence and vocal art, Miss Anderson stamped herself in the memory and the lasting esteem of those who attended. At the end of the act, the audience could not have enough of Miss Anderson, recalling her again and again before the curtain.

But, as Downes wrote on another occasion, "It is fifteen years late for Miss Anderson to be recognized by the Met," and it is not in opera but in recital that we shall remember her. We shall see her standing, erect in the curve of the piano, a figure of dignity, even royalty, her hands clasped, her eyes often closed, singing perhaps Schubert's "Ave Maria" or "He's Got the Whole World in His Hands."

She had, as Marcia Davenport wrote, a pair of voices. "The upper half . . . brilliant and flexible and heady, a soprano for all technical and interpretive purposes . . . the lower half . . . that hair-raising, deep voice, the like of which I have never heard, and which, I suspect, has never been heard before. In such songs as 'Der Erlkoenig' or 'Der Tod und das Maedchen,' which consist of conversations between two voices, a high one and a low one, she is amazing." But many felt that she was at her best when she sang the religious songs of her own people. "That," Virgil Thomson wrote, "is where she leaves off being a lovely icicle and becomes a flame."

The world's adulation never destroyed her humility and graciousness. She always retained, in the words of one critic, "the simplicity of the truly great," while the novelist Fannie Hurst observed that "she had grown great simply." With her the use of the third person in speaking of herself was not an affectation but the mark of modesty.

In countless thousands of Negro homes, a picture of Marian Anderson hangs on the wall. No one can guess how many Black children, both girls and boys, have taken singing lessons in the hope of being like her. She helped to open many doors.

After her farewell recital on Easter Sunday, 1965, she sang once more, in Sainte-Chapelle in Paris, to raise funds for the Festival of Negro Arts at Dakar. She has appeared with many major orchestras in a non-singing role, usually the narrator in Copland's *A Lincoln Portrait*, but most of her time has been spent at Marianna Farm, her Connecticut home, in a house designed by her husband, the architect, Orpheus Fisher. She is active in many good causes, including most recently the campaign to save Town Hall, where she made her debut more than fifty years ago. As the *New York Times* said in an editorial following her farewell recital: "Marian Anderson will never be able to retire from being one of the world's great ladies."

22   Paul Robeson, the Singer

It is very difficult for the professional music critic to evaluate the singing of the late Paul Robeson. He possessed one of the most beautiful vocal instruments ever produced by this country. But in matters of technique, musicianship, and style, he never became a complete master.

As he stated to the press many times, Robeson wanted only to be an artist of the people. With the exception of a few art songs by Schubert and Moussorgsky and an occasional operatic aria, he devoted his programs to the folk songs of the world's people.

He was one of the first concert artists to present an entire program of Black American folk music. This historical event took place on Sunday, April 19, 1925, at the Greenwich Village Theatre, with Lawrence Brown at the piano. Public and critics alike found it an overwhelming experience.

After one performance of *Boris Godunov* by the Metropolitan Opera I listened to my recording of Robeson both reciting the text and singing an excerpt from this opera. It was indeed a great loss to the operatic world that we never heard him in this role on stage.[3]

Paul Robeson was a celebrity before he sang a note or stepped onto a stage. His fame began at Rutgers where he won twelve varsity letters and was twice named to Walter Camp's All-American Football team. He also achieved Phi Beta Kappa in his junior year. (But he failed to make the Rutgers Glee Club!)

After graduation in 1919 he went to Columbia Law School and practiced law briefly in a New York office. In 1921, however, he married Eslanda Cardozo Goode, who urged him to try the stage, where his rich voice and commanding presence promised rich rewards.

Beginning with an amateur production of *Simon the Cyrenian* at the Harlem YMCA, he quickly made it to Broadway. The show was *Taboo*, and it included a song by Harry T. Burleigh. Heywood Broun wrote in his review that he did not understand the story, but "it seemed of little consequence as long as Paul L. Robeson was singing." After Broadway, the play, renamed *Voodoo* was produced in London, with Robeson co-starring with Mrs. Patrick Campbell. That was his first visit to England, which later became his home for many years.

Back in New York, he substituted for a time in *Shuffle Along* and sang J. Rosamond Johnson's "L'il Gal" at the Plantation where Florence Mills was the star. Meantime, Eugene O'Neill had seen Robeson act and had written *All God's Chillun Got Wings* with him in mind. The production by the Provincetown Players in Greenwich Village was a success, and so O'Neill's *Emperor Jones* was revived for him. George Jean Nathan described Robeson as "one of the most thoroughly eloquent, impressive, and convincing actors" he had ever seen.

There is a scene where Brutus Jones, lost in the jungle, is supposed to whistle to keep up his courage. But Robeson's whistling apparently wasn't very good, so it was decided that he should sing a spiritual instead and the effect was tremendous.

That led directly to his first recital, one of the historic events in the chronicle of Blacks in music. The date was April 19, 1925; the place was the Greenwich Village Theatre —sold out for the occasion. Lawrence Brown was the accompanist and collaborator. Except for one group made up of songs by Avery Robinson, J. Rosamond Johnson, Will Marion Cook, and Burleigh, the program was devoted entirely to Negro spirituals, and its purpose was to show off this major contribution of Blacks to the world's music.

The critic of the *New York World* observed that the audience "may have been present at a turning point—one of those thin points of time when a star is born. It is a voice in which deep bells ring. It is not trained, but it has all it needs— perfect pace, beautiful enunciation." Robeson, said the *Times*, "is a singer of genuine power. The voice is ample for his needs, mellow and soft, but it is his intense earnestness which grips his hearers . . . it is the cry from the depths, the universal humanism, that touches the heart . . . they voiced the sorrows and hopes of a people." So great was the public interest, that the concert had to be repeated the next Sunday.

He was subjected to incidences of discrimination. When the Metropolitan Opera produced the Louis Gruenberg opera based on *Emperor Jones*, which opened on January 7, 1933. Robeson, who had played the O'Neill drama hunreds of times and whose singing was by then acclaimed throughout the world, was not invited to sing the role. Instead, the honor went to Lawrence Tibbett—who did very well the critics agreed—but Brutus Jones is a black man. Olin Downes, noting Robeson's "exceptional endowment as a singer and dramatic interpreter," lamented, "He would have been a highly impressive Boris or Mefistofele or Emperor Jones."

While the Met was closed to him, Robeson did sing excerpts from *Emperor Jones* with the Philadelphia Orchestra under Ormandy at Carnegie Hall, December 18, 1940. "Mr. Robeson became at once the speaking and singing actor and drove every word of text and song home," wrote Downes in the *Times*. (It should be noted that Jules Bledsoe did sing the actual opera in 1934 in Europe and later that year in New York with the Aeolian Opera Association, a Black opera company.)

In November 1929, Robeson established himself as one of the great drawing cards of the musical world when he sang two sold-out recitals in Carnegie Hall only five days apart. This began a fifteen-year period that marked the height of the Robeson career. In 1930 he went to London to do the first of many productions of Shakespeare's *Othello*. The Broadway production in 1943 with Uta Hagen and Jose Ferrer ran 296 performances, at that time an American record for a Shakespeare play. He sang "Ol' Man River" in the

London production of *Show Boat* and in the famous 1932 American revival and the 1936 film. (Bledsoe sang the original American production.) He appeared frequently on radio, climaxed by his introduction of Earl Robinson's "Ballad for Americans" on a national broadcast in 1939, a frequently repeated staple of his recital programs that meant more then in the face of the threat of Hitler's Germany than it does now. He starred in eleven films, including *Emperor Jones* and *Show Boat*. (In 1924 he had appeared in a Black-produced film, *Body and Soul*, which was shown only in Black communities.) Most of his three hundred recordings came out during this period. One worth noting is Robeson singing the blues with Count Basie's band. Blues was of course another form of Negro folk music. "Having a good voice is no disqualification for singing the blues," noted one critic.

Robeson, believing his music belonged to the people, frequently sang outdoor concerts before mammoth audiences. Thirty thousand crowded Hollywood Bowl in 1940, probably the largest number it ever held. One hundred fifty thousand gathered in Grant Park, Chicago, the same year. Twenty thousand heard him at Lewisohn Stadium in New York in 1943.

Yet within a few years after these outpourings of public adulation, his career virtually stopped; concert halls were closed to him; he was reviled as a traitor to the country of his birth; and he was reduced to singing before radical Communist-front groups. His political views, developed over the years and never concealed, cannot be separated from his artistry—both had a common foundation. His own father had been a slave. The celebrity that Robeson achieved only emphasized the slights which, like every Black, he experienced, and he was always able to identify with the mass of Blacks who were not shielded from oppression by the accident of fame. The deep feeling he brought to the spirituals and other Black music derived from this identification with the fight for Black freedom. In leaning toward radical remedies, he reflected the hopelessness that at that time seemed to surround the Black cause.

By the late 1950s the bitter clouds of McCarthyism had begun to lift; Robeson's passport, taken from him in 1950, was returned; concert halls again opened their doors to him. Carnegie Hall was filled when he returned on May 9, 1958, after a decade's absence, and the recital had to be repeated two weeks later. It turned out that this was Robeson's last New York recital. He gave several more in Europe, but he never sang again after becoming ill in 1961.

Robeson was always realistic about his strengths and weaknesses as a recitalist. "I am essentially a folk song singer," he said. "I am not especially at home with Brahms or Schumann." And on another occasion, "I have never been much interested in vocal virtuosity. I have never tried to sing an A-flat while the audience held on the edge of its collective seat to see if I could make it." But what he could do has never been done better. The resonance, the sonority, the clarity, the expressiveness he brought to the spirituals (and other folk songs) made of them an art form worthy of the concert hall.

On April 17, 1973, Robeson filled Carnegie Hall for the last time. The occasion was the celebration of his seventy-fifth birthday—but this time he could not be present. He sent a tape on which he said, "I am still the same Paul, dedicated as ever to the worldwide cause of humanity for freedom, peace, and brotherhood." Less than three years later, on January 23, 1976, he died.

The controversy that surrounded him much of his life has

been stilled, and we can remember him not alone as one of America's great singers but also as one of America's great men.

23   Roland Hayes's Children

The great success on the concert stage of Roland Hayes, Marian Anderson, and Paul Robeson was a source of inspiration to many later Black singers. But it was the artistry of Hayes—the supreme interpreter and stylist—which became the yardstick by which future artists would measure themselves.

Soprano Dorothy Maynor was the first of these to emerge as a major artist. When she auditioned in 1939 for Serge Koussevitzky at Tanglewood, he is said to have exclaimed: "The whole world must hear her!" Critic Noel Strauss spread the news around the country.

When she made her Town Hall debut on November 19, 1939, a large audience greeted her with great expectation. Her program included the music of Bach, Handel, Schubert, Wolf, Strauss, and a group of Afro-American spirituals. It was designed to show off her best qualities.

Olin Downes of the *New York Times* reported: "For Miss Maynor's voice is phenomenal for its range, character, and varied expressive resources. It is equally adapted to music of a lyric or dramatic character. The voice has power as well as rich color."

She immediately began a career that took her around the country for recitals and appearances as soloist with most of the leading orchestras. She was engaged by RCA Victor to make some of the recordings that have preserved for posterity the glory of her early singing.

By 1942, her voice began to lose some of its beauty, and Virgil Thomson was forced to report in the *Herald Tribune*: "There can be no further question, I think, that her vocal technique is woefully inadequate and that her voice itself is in danger."

Her recording legacy is another matter. No one has sung on records a more exquisite performance of "Depuis le Jour" from *Louise*. And her singing of Schubert's "Der Hirt auf dem Felsen" is unsurpassed. These moments are ours to enjoy and savor for many years to come.

When I was a student at the Academy of Music and Dramatic Art in Vienna in 1960, I received a touching letter from the great soprano Ellabelle Davis. It began: "I have been oooh so sick. . . ." Soon after, I read in the newspaper that she had died on November 15, 1960.

Thus ended a career which began with a highly praised Town Hall debut on October 25, 1942. The *Herald Tribune* reported: "Her voice is of extraordinarily persuasive texture, gleaming limpidity through its wide range. She has an innate musicality and sense of style found only in the true artist."

She began to sing recitals and appear with major orchestras throughout the United States, Latin America, and Europe. She also made a brief excursion into opera, singing the title role in *Aida* in Mexico City as well as in Santiago, Chile, with considerable success.

One of the important moments in her career came when The League of Composers commissioned a work for her from Lukas Foss entitled *The Song of Songs*. She sang its pre-

WILLIAM GRANT STILL

FLORENCE PRICE

ROLAND HAYES

MARIAN ANDERSON

PAUL ROBESON

ZELMA GEORGE

JESSYE NORMAN

Left: LEONTYNE PRICE

NATALIE HINDERAS

ANDRE WATTS

KERMIT MOORE

SANFORD ALLEN

Left: DEAN DIXON

HENRY LEWIS

EVA JESSYE

miere with the Boston Symphony under Koussevitzky in 1947, after which she sang it with many other orchestras.

I first heard Miss Davis when she sang a recital of German Lieder at the Kaufman Auditorium of the YM-YWHA in the 1950s. Her program included Schumann's *"Frauenliebe und Leben* as well as songs by Schubert, Wolf, and Strauss. She was assisted by Arpad Sandor at the piano.

Especially memorable was the group of Wolf Lieder, each sharply etched in terms of vocal characterization. As far as technique was concerned, there was not one note out of place. She had a voice of extraordinary beauty, always placed at the service of the music.

In 1944, contralto Carol Brice became the first Black to win the coveted Naumburg Award. Her Town Hall debut on March 13, 1945, was greeted with great critical acclaim. The *Herald Tribune* found her "gifted with a sumptuous voice which she employs with considerable skill."

Throughout her numerous concert tours in the late forties and fifties, Miss Brice was accompanied on the piano by her brother, Jonathan, a remarkable musician in his own right. During the sixties, she made operatic appearances with the New York City Opera.

Her recording of Manuel de Falla's spine-tingling *El Amor Brujo* with Fritz Reiner conducting The Pittsburgh Symphony on Columbia exploits her ravishing chest tones. She can also be heard on an unusually fine recording of Mahler's cycle *Lieder eines fahrenden Gesellen.*

I first heard baritone William Warfield in the title role in *Porgy and Bess* in the fifties at the National Theatre in Washington, D.C. At that time, I was impressed as much with his acting as with his deep-throated singing and looked forward to hearing him in recital.

I was not among those fortunate enough to be present at his sensational Town Hall debut on March 19, 1950. At that time, the *Herald Tribune* reported that he was "endowed with a phenomenal voice which he projected with complete artistry throughout a long, highly exacting program."

One of the remarkable things about Warfield is his versatility. He is at home in the straight dramatic role of De Lawd in *The Green Pastures*. And he is able to sing the music of Joe in *Show Boat* with the majesty of an operatic aria.

The opportunity came for me to hear him in a recital on February 14, 1965, at Carnegie Hall. It was a typical Warfield program, starting with unusual items by Purcell and Handel, the *Four Serious Songs* by Brahms, and a group of spirituals on the Passion theme arranged by Roland Hayes.

The second half of the program consisted of Loewe and Schubert songs, Ravel's *Don Quichotte a Dulcinée* and the first performance of John Carter's *Saetas profanas*. Everything was sung with such great conviction that one forgot that Warfield's voice was beginning to show some wear.

Unfortunately, I have lost a copy of the review I wrote for the Associated Negro Press, but I remember roughly what I said. I suggested that, if William Warfield had been born in early times in Nuremberg, he would have been crowned as a *Meistersinger*. I still hold that view.

When I arrived in New York twenty-five years ago, all of my musical friends were talking about a new soprano named Adele Addison. She had just made her Town Hall debut on January 16, 1952, and she set critical minds on a search for new adjectives to describe her artistry.

One wrote: "a truly beautiful voice of pearly lustre and clarity, a generous share of warmth and feeling and good looks. Equally important, she has complemented them with enough intelligence to make her singing artistically effective." The others were equally ecstatic.

I later heard her debut with the New York City Opera in the role of Mimi in *La Boheme* on March 27, 1955, and found that all of the superlatives I had heard relating to her singing were quite true. Added to these, she also turned out to be a singing actress of great distinction.

When I finally got to hear her give a recital at Town Hall, she offered a very exacting program including Schumann's *Frauenliebe und Leben*. What struck me most on that occasion was the wonderful sense of joy she radiated while she set about the task of singing.

Another artist who also seems to get much personal satisfaction while performing is mezzo-soprano Betty Allen, who made her Town Hall debut on January 7, 1958. She offered Brahms' Songs for Alto, Viola and Piano and revealed a voice with the richness and vibrancy of a fine cello.

During her long career as a singer, she has sung with many of the best orchestras under the great conductors. And she has sung opera. Of her appearance in *The Young Lord*, one critic wrote: "Miss Allen's personality is such that at least two stages are needed to contain her."

24   The Road to the Met

When Sidney Poitier became the first Black to receive the Academy Award as best actor in 1963, he said: "It has been a long journey to this moment." This sentiment must have been shared by the first Black singers who made the long journey to the stage of the Metropolitan Opera.

According to James Weldon Johnson in his book *Black Manhattan* (New York: Alfred A. Knopf, 1930), Sissieretta Jones (Black Patti) was given a contract to sing at the Metropolitan Opera in 1892 by Abbey, Schoeffel, and Grau. A fire closed the house down soon after, and her debut never took place.

A giant step was made in the direction of the Met by soprano Caterina Jarboro when she became the first Black woman to sing with a major American company. She sang the title role in *Aida* with Alfredo Salmaggi's Chicago Opera Company in New York's Hippodrome in 1933.

Another important moment was the debut of baritone Todd Duncan in *Pagliacci* at the New York City Opera on September 28, 1945. He was the first Black singer to appear with that company and the first in operatic history to sing a so-called "white" role.

Francis D. Perkins reported in the *New York Herald Tribune*: "His singing of the prologue was very musicianly, especially in its phrasing and expressive sensitiveness. His voice is pleasing in its timbre and color and was ably employed."

Duncan also played Escamillo in *Carmen.*

The first Black woman to become a regular member of an American opera company was soprano Camilla Williams. When she sang the role of Cio-Cio-San in *Madama Butterfly* on May 15, 1946, with the New York City Opera, she made headlines in newspapers throughout the country.

In *P.M.*, Robert A. Hague wrote: "She produced some full and brilliant high notes in the first-act love duet which brought down the house, and there was another ovation after her beautifully voiced 'One Fine Day.' " Miss Williams went on to make a brilliant career in opera and concert.

For singers, the real prelude to the Metropolitan Opera came when bass-baritone Fred Thomas won first place in the annual "Auditions of the Air" in March of 1951. That same year, he made his Town Hall debut. The *Herald Tribune* reported that he "gave an impression of poise and musicianship."

But it was contralto Marian Anderson who, according to *Variety*, "like Joshua, but more quietly, had fought the battle of Jericho and at last the walls came tumbling down." On January 7, 1955, she made her Metropolitan Opera debut as Ulrica in *The Masked Ball.* The door was opened at last.

I was a witness to Miss Anderson's debut that night, and I am grateful that I did not have to review the performance. It was a shattering emotional experience that made me want both to shout with joy and cry at the same time. It was a great moment in operatic history.

Three weeks later, on January 28, 1955, baritone Robert McFerrin made his debut as Amonasro in *Aida* at the Met, thus becoming the first Black male to join the company. A winner of the 1953 auditions, he subsequently trained in the Kathryn Turney Long School.

The *New York Times* wrote: "In Mr. McFerrin, he (Mr. Bing) has found a baritone with a warm, smooth, supple voice. It is a voice solidly in focus and it has fine, ringing top tones. Vocally, Mr. McFerrin will do all right." He went on to sing the title role in *Rigoletto* among others.

The first Black leading soprano to sing at the Metropolitan Opera was Mattiwilda Dobbs, who had already graced the stages of major European houses. On November 9, 1956, she made her debut as Gilda in *Rigoletto*, a role which she had previously sung only in English.

In the *New York World-Telegram and Sun*, Louis Biancolli wrote: "By any standards Miss Dobbs is a remarkable artist, very much in the tradition of great coloraturas in that her phrasing and shading are fully as fascinating as her breathtaking agility in the upper register."

The first Black tenor to sing with the company was George Shirley, who made his debut in the role of Ferrando in *Cosi Fan Tutte* on October 24, 1961. That same year he had won the auditions as well as a contract. His debut was as a replacement for an ailing colleague.

Harold C. Schonberg of the *New York Times* reported: "Mr. Shirley, giving little indication of the strain under which he must have been laboring, displayed a flexible light tenor voice of very appealing quality." Shirley continued to sing leading roles with the company for over a decade.

Now, the roster of the Metropolitan, as well as of all the major opera houses of the world, boasts a number of fine Black singing actors. The Black male singer is still less visible than one might like. But, to return to Sidney Poitier's words: "It has been a long journey to this moment."

25 Zelma George Integrates Broadway

Zelma Watson George of Cleveland, Ohio, became the first Negro woman to play a leading "white" role on Broadway on Wednesday, July 19, 1950 in Gian Carlo Menotti's opera *The Medium*. Sold out long in advance, the event took place in the Arena Theatre of the Edison Hotel.

Before coming to Broadway, Mrs. George played the role of Madam Flora sixty-seven times at Karamu Theatre. Word of her overwhelming success in Cleveland reached the composer and he personally invited her to star in this revival under his supervision.

Although she studied voice at the American Conservatory of Music in Chicago, Mrs. George had distinguished herself as a sociologist, musicologist, and lecturer. Married to Clayborne George, president of the Cleveland Civil Service Commission, this was her first operatic venture.

The opening night audience was stunned by the vocal and dramatic power of her performance. Mrs. George, who played the role in a wheelchair, was especially effective in her delivery of the aria "Afraid, Madam Flora, Afraid." It was sung with chilling intensity.

Evelyn Keller and Leo Coleman repeated their well-known portrayals of Monica and Toby, respectively. The fine cast also included Derna de Lys as Mrs. Gobineau, Paul King as Mr. Gobineau, and Dorothy Staiger as Mrs. Nolan. A two-piano reduction of the orchestral score was used.

Opening this double bill was Menotti's short opera *The Telephone*, with Edith Gordon as Lucy and Paul King as Ben. This slight piece never fails to charm, even though it is hardly in the same league with *The Medium*. It served to whet the appetite for the main course.

But this was clearly Zelma George's evening. With the final chord of *The Medium*, the audience rose to its feet cheering. This ovation must have resounded all over Broadway. It was a fitting tribute to a great singing actress in one of the great roles in American operatic repertory.[4]

The late Langston Hughes once described Dr. Zelma George as "a woman of many parts." She has distinguished herself in so many different areas that it would take a volume to catalogue her achievements. After her appearance in *The Medium* in New York, she returned home to Cleveland, where she recreated the role of the Mother in Gian Carlo Menotti's opera *The Consul* at the Cleveland Play House, and Mrs. Peacham in Kurt Weill's *The Threepenny Opera* at Karamu Theatre.

Perhaps her most important musical achievement was her extraordinary thesis "A Guide to Negro Music: An Annotated Bibliography of Negro Folk Music and Art Music by Negro Composers or Based on Negro Thematic Material." It includes 12,163 titles of Negro music and literature about it and is permanently housed in the Howard University library. This document is indispensable to anyone involved in research on Black music.

Another great performance that deserves special recognition was that of soprano Muriel Rahn in the Jan Meyerowitz–Langston Hughes opera *The Barrier*, which received its premiere at Columbia University in 1950. The *New York Times* wrote: "Muriel Rahn, who sang the title role in *Carmen Jones* on Broadway, sings Cora and gives a stunning performance. She brings a personal dignity and sincerity to the part, and her singing is not only accurate and full-bodied, but charged with dramatic cogency. Miss Rahn's Cora is the core of the piece—its fire and artistic conscience."

26   Debut Recital: Leontyne Price

In a review for the Associated Negro Press dated November 19, 1954, I wrote:

"Soprano Leontyne Price made her much anticipated New York recital debut at Town Hall on Sunday, November 14. Word of her great successes in *Four Saints in Three Acts* and *Porgy and Bess* had aroused the curiosity of local concert-goers and they filled the hall to capacity.

"Her program was a model of taste and refinement. It included less familiar works by Gluck, Rossini, Stravinsky, Haieff, and Mahler. And it offered the first New York performances of Samuel Barber's Hermit Songs as well as of songs by Manuel Rosenthal.

"Miss Price is, without question, a major talent. She possesses a voice of exceptional beauty with a wide range. The slight tremulo that was ever present seemed to be the result of debut nerves. But, for the most part, she was in complete command of her vocal resources.

"She seemed most at home in the Barber cycle, which is

based on texts by Irish monks from the eighth to the twelfth centuries. She captured the essence of each text and projected it to the audience simply and directly. Her English diction was exemplary. The composer accompanied her at the piano.

"Because they require an instrumental approach, the Mahler songs also suited Miss Price quite well. She captured the contemplative mood in 'Ich bin der Welt abhanden gekommen' and brought out the gentle humour of 'Wer hat dies Liedlein erdacht?' David Stimer's accompaniments were fine. In fact, everything on the program was well planned and executed. It will take some time before Miss Price acquires that special personal identification with her material that is the mark of a true Lieder singer. This listener will be watching her progress with great interest."

This recital was but another step in the spectacular rise of Miss Price to the position she now holds in the music world —*prima donna assoluta*. It was followed by a series of carefully planned debuts in the great opera houses of the world, each leading up to the ultimate goal, the Met.

These were: her debut with the NBC-TV Opera Company in the title role in *Tosca* in 1955; her debut at the Vienna State Opera under Herbert von Karajan in 1958; and her debut at La Scala in 1960. Reports of her triumphs reached New York by way of ample coverage in the press.

So, when she finally reached the stage of the Metropolitan Opera for her debut as Leonora in *Il Trovatore* on January 27, 1961, interest had been built up to the point of frenzy. At the opera's conclusion, she received a forty-two-minute ovation, one of the longest in the company's history.

This kind of stormy ovation is the rule when Miss Price appears, whether it be in opera or on the concert stage. As I pointed out in a recent review, it must be very difficult indeed for her to regain concentration and subject her voice and temperament to the needs of the music.

But Miss Price is an artist of great integrity. She meticulously prepares herself for each assignment, leaving no stone left unturned. And it is a tribute to her artistry that, after the hysteria has subsided, she allows the message of the composer to shine through.

27   Martina Arroyo: A Conversation

It would take a round-the-world trip to keep up with Harlem-born soprano Martina Arroyo. If you miss her at New York's Metropolitan Opera, you might catch up with her in Milan at Teatro alla Scala, in London at the Royal Opera, in Vienna at the Staatsoper, or in Buenos Aires at Teatro Colon. Or you might find her singing with the Cleveland Orchestra, Boston Symphony, or even as a guest on "The Tonight Show" on TV. Wherever she is, you can be sure of one thing—she will be the *prima donna*, which is opera's term for the leading lady. Here are some excerpts from a recent conversation in her Manhattan apartment.

Arroyo: I don't know if you remember, but you were in on the very beginning of my career. When I first met you, I was doing a concert in Vienna for Amerika-Haus. That's how I got started—singing Lieder and oratorio. I think that this has had an influence on my life as an opera singer. This means that I pull out of the opera scene every now and then to do a concert. I think that it keeps the voice fresh and keeps me in contact with another musical form.

Abdul: In a sense, you have to create a different character for each song, is that not so?

Arroyo: Right. And you also try to bring something of your approach to Lieder into opera. Of course, opera is done on a grander scale. Distance makes a difference, and the effect one colleague has on another also plays a great part.

Abdul: How do you feel about the relationship between the Black singer and the type of roles he plays?

Arroyo: To me, being Black is not a problem. Perhaps you have to know a little more about make-up, but otherwise one is concerned with the same problems as one's white colleagues. How can you use *your* qualities for the characterization and make it work? This is my main concern.

Abdul: Among the roles you have played at the Metropolitan, I notice that Elsa in *Lohengrin* is included. Since Elsa is a symbol of white womanhood, I am curious as to how you handled the visual problem?

Arroyo: For many people it came as a shock that Elsa worked better for me than many of the so-called "Black" roles. Some people thought Mr. Bing had lost his mind when he cast me in the role. He went with me to the dressmaking department and tried the costumes on me and made the slight changes that made all the difference in the world. Instead of putting me in white and silver, he put me in white and gold. It still gave the so-called "white" look, but with the gold hues with my soft-toned skin, I gave the same impression, which wouldn't have worked for me with the silver. It just took a bit of extra thinking and came out with the same results.

Abdul: What happens when you learn a role with a director in one house and then move on to another house and work with a different director?

Arroyo: This happened with *The Masked Ball* one season.

When I sang the role at the San Francisco Opera, the director did some incredible things with the staging. Shortly afterward, I had to work at the Chicago Lyric Opera with another director. I found myself using some of the things that I had learned from San Francisco.

Abdul: What suggestions would you give a young person just starting out in the business?

Arroyo: It depends on what you mean by *young*. You have to be very careful that you don't hurt the voice before it matures. Of course, your choice of teachers is the biggest problem of your entire career. If your voice has not yet reached maturity, I would suggest the study of a string instrument and the piano. The string instrument helps in training the ear and in the learning of intervals. Then, get as much repertoire as you can—listening to all kinds of music by going to concerts. And don't leave out popular music. You can get some of the most beautiful phrasing in the world from listening to Roberta Flack. Another thing is not to sing the wrong things too early. Allow the voice to grow naturally. Start learning old Italian songs and Lieder. Learn about line, about *legato*. You can learn these things before the voice matures, because what you will be doing is developing it and helping it to grow without pushing. You can push a voice in the wrong direction and ruin a good instrument. During this early period, you can learn your languages and about the characters in opera.

Abdul: What do you think about television as a source of learning?

Arroyo: It can be a great source of information and strength in the home. Of course, you must be selective. You can see such things as Nureyev and Fonteyn. And televised opera. Can you imagine what it's like to bring opera close up so people can see the development of the characters right in their own home? What young people today have at their disposal is so incredible. You can be like a sponge and soak all of this up, or you can let it keep you from growing if you let it. I'd love to be fifteen again and be starting out with all of these resources at my disposal.

28   Miss Bumbry's Met Debut

On Thursday evening, October 7, 1965, the dazzling new mezzo soprano Miss Grace Bumbry, a native of St. Louis, made her Metropolitan debut as Princess Eboli in Verdi's *Don Carlo*. The capacity audience rewarded her with three solo curtain calls. This is rare indeed in an opera house where most of the world's greatest singers have sung.

It was apparent from her entrance that Miss Bumbry was star material. She swept in on cue and paused majestically for that extra split second that marks a star from a run of the mill debutante. The audience burst into a stormy ovation before she had sung one note.

And when she sang the fiendishly difficult aria "Canzone De Velo," which requires the mezzo to sing with the flexibility of a coloratura, Miss Bumbry tossed it off as if it were the easiest task in the world for her. This only served to whet the audience's appetite for what was to come.

Miss Bumbry's big moment came in the third act when she sang the famous "O, Don Fatale." Here she exploited her remarkable range, deep chest tones, creamy middle voice, and soaring high tones—all beautifully equalized and technically secure. She also proved to be a superb actress.

There is much more to *Don Carlo* than Princess Eboli and her scenes. It is a great musical drama concerning itself with the Spanish Inquisition, based on a tragedy by Schiller. On this occasion, the balance of the cast was made up of some very distinguished artists. They were: Jerome Hines as Philip I, Bruno Prevedi as the Don, Ettore Bastianini as Rodrigo, and Raina Kabalvanska as Elizabeth of Valois. The excellent conductor was Thomas Schippers. But this was Miss Bumbry's evening, and she made the most of it.[5]

Miss Bumbry's dramatic entry into the operatic arena took place in 1961 when she became the first Black to sing a major role at the Bayreuth Festival. Her appearance as Venus in *Tannhäuser* provoked a storm of protest from the "purists," but it ended in a personal triumph and international headlines.

In recent times, she has been singing soprano roles such as Tosca, Salome, and Lady Macbeth. In an interview recently in New York, Miss Bumbry reminded me that she started out as a soprano and that, when she sang Venus at Bayreuth, it was the Dresden version—for soprano.

29   Miss Verrett as Lady Macbeth

Teatro alla Scala of Milan is known to cognoscenti as the home of Italian opera style. Since many definitive performances of Giuseppe Verdi operas have emanated from La Scala, his *Macbeth* was an excellent choice to open its first U.S. season at the Kennedy Center on Tuesday evening, September 7, 1976.

In spite of the appearance of the Black American soprano Shirley Verrett as Lady Macbeth, this was not a special export product. It was the same production seen in Milan during the 1975–1976 season staged by Giorgio Strehler, designed by Luciano Damiani, and conducted by Claudio Abbado.

Verdi once wrote his publisher Ricordi and insisted that *Macbeth* never be allowed to be performed at La Scala. He wrote: "I have examples enough to persuade me that here they don't know how, or don't want, to put on operas, and especially my operas, as they should be put on."

If it had been possible for Verdi to see this production at the Kennedy Center, I think that he would have been very pleased—with a few reservations. Above all, his music was allowed to shine through without distortion, and this was due to the scrupulous musical direction of Claudio Abbado.

The opera itself has some static moments that present problems to interpreters. Verdi himself was fully aware of this, and he revised the score and its weak libretto by Francesco Maria Piave for the first Paris revival. The La Scala production uses the revised score.

Stage director Strehler and his designer Damiani have chosen to concern themselves with the overall mood of the piece. Consequently, the setting was quite bare (so was Shakespeare's), and the lighting was dark and foreboding. The principals needed more light during their arias.

But the true test of the leading singers is in their singing of the arias. Piero Cappuccilli (Macbeth) followed Verdi's instructions to "*cantare in sordina*" (sing with muted effect) in his soliloquy "Is This a Dagger?" and the effect was shattering.

It was Miss Verrett's reading of Lady Macbeth's sleepwalking scene that really stopped the show. While balancing precariously on a ledge, she delivered her aria moving slowly from one side of the stage to the other. She used a dazzling array of vocal colors to express what was in the music.

There has been some concern from observers of the vocal scene over the transition from mezzo to soprano repertoire on the part of Miss Verrett. Because she is a superb vocal technician with a wide range, there seemed to be no cause for real concern at this time. She handled it magnificently.

Special mention should be made of the unusually fine chorus and orchestra of Teatro alla Scala. Maestro Abbado kept such a firm control over the entire proceedings that, more than once, I had the impression that this was really a concert version of the opera.

This was an historic occasion, cause for great celebration. Some of my colleagues from the New York press were less than enthusiastic in their reviews. Perhaps what New York needs is a strong cool breeze to sweep away some of the cobwebs in critical minds.[6]

I first heard Shirley Verrett as a recitalist, the occasion being her Town Hall debut in 1958 as a Naumburg Award winner. Even then, it was evident that she not only had a voice of extraordinary beauty, but also all of the instincts of a Lieder singer par excellence.

Now at the peak of her career, she devotes most of her attention to the operatic stage in both soprano and mezzo roles. Just before the La Scala appearance in Washington, she sang *Norma* on the Metropolitan Opera's tour. After her triumph with La Scala, she opened the Met season as Azucena.

30   Prelude to Isolde

Pierre Boulez, musical director of the New York Phil-harmonic, offered a deeply satisfying program of works by Bela Bartok, Alban Berg, and Richard Wagner on Thursday evening, January 20, 1977, at Avery Fisher Hall. Most of the material focused on less familiar aspects of each composer's musical profile.

The choice of Berg's concert aria "Der Wein" (1929) was timely, in view of the fact that the Metropolitan Opera was about to mount that composer's opera *Lulu.* These settings of three Baudelaire poems (in the Stefan George German translation) reflect the same spirit as that of the opera.

Soprano Jessye Norman was the soloist. In view of the complex nature of the score, it was only natural that she occupied herself more with musical rather than textual matters. Her dark, rich voice soared easily over the orchestra.

She was also heard in Wagner's five Wesendonk Lieder, which came out of the composer's *Tristan* period. These poems by Mathilde Wesendonk (1828–1902), with whom Wagner had an affair, were originally written for voice and piano. The orchestrations used were by Felix Mottle.

Miss Norman has become a specialist in the interpretation of these songs, having recorded them on the Philips label. On this occasion, she not only sang them magnificently, but moved us deeply by her complete identification with the texts.[7]

❖   ❖   ❖

The appearances of Jessye Norman seem all to point to an Isolde—the first Black one. Besides singing the Wesendonk Lieder, she has recorded Isolde's "Liebestod" on Philips (9500-031) with Colin Davis and the London Symphony Orchestra.

Her voice is every bit as glorious as that of Kirsten Flagstad, only warmer, and her communication of the text is remarkable. Like her predessesor, Miss Norman is also a superb recitalist. She has an excellent command of German and French, and her song interpretations have style and elegance.

31   A Pair of Sopranos

Two fine sopranos made important appearances in New York in May, 1976. Clamma Dale made her long-awaited recital debut at Alice Tully Hall under the auspices of the Walter W. Naumburg Foundation on Monday, May 3. Joyce Britton offered a song program at Carnegie Recital Hall on Wednesday, May 5.

Blessed with a velvet smooth voice, Miss Dale revealed all of the elements that can be moulded into a major career. This was especially true in her performance of the *Cantos del Tucuman* by the Argentinian composer Alberto Ginastera in which she was assisted by an excellent instrumental ensemble.

But, in a group of Schubert Lieder, certain inconsistencies in vocal method were apparent and these could lead to problems at a later date. The sounds were never less than pretty, however, and she understands correct Schubert performance style.

She needs to work on her German diction, especially the

ch sounds and final *r*'s. There was no sense of the drama so essential to the success of "Die junge Nonne," and this was due in great part to the colorless piano accompaniment by Neil Stannard.

In a group of songs by Gabriel Fauré, Miss Dale sang well and brought out the subtle meaning in the phrase "Qu'as-tu fait, o toi que voilà, de ta jeunesse?" in "Prison." The highlight of an American group was Norman Dello Joio's "New Born," magnificently sung.

Joyce Britton, a native of Jamaica, West Indies, took a long time in warming up her fine voice, but our patience was rewarded. She has that nice, crystal clear sound one associates with Erna Berger and extraordinarily fine German diction.

One of the highlights of the program was a performance of Schubert's "Der Hirt auf dem Felsen." She was given wonderful support by her superb accompanist (really musical partner), Mikael Eliasen, and clarinetist Larry Guy, who played from memory.

I was disturbed by a lack of animation on the part of the singer, a lack of what I call "humor." This might be due to the fact that Miss Britton may not be singing publicly often enough these days. In any case, it was good to have her back on the New York stage.[8]

32   Four Outstanding Sopranos

Four Black sopranos made important appearances in concert and opera in November 1976. Kathleen Battle and Faye Robinson assumed major roles with the New York City

Opera. Leontyne Price was soloist with the Berlin Philharmonic, and Barbara Hendricks made her local recital debut.

At the Saturday matinee, November 13, at the New York City Opera, Miss Battle stepped into the role of Susanna in an excellent production of Mozart's *The Marriage of Figaro*. She possesses a light, perfectly schooled voice and the stage presence of a veteran singing actress.

There was much speculation over the casting of Miss Robinson in the role of Violetta in the company's production of Verdi's *La Traviata* on Sunday evening, November 14. This was the second time in the history of opera in America that a Black had been seen in this role.

On March 29, 1944, Mme. Lillian Evanti (Lillian Evans Tibbs) was Violetta in the National Negro Opera Company's production at Madison Square Garden. At that time, Virgil Thomson wrote in the *New York Herald Tribune* that she "has a voice of wide range and many colors."

When Miss Robinson sang "Sempre Libera" so fully and splendidly in the first act on Sunday, it was hard to believe that this was the same woman who would die of consumption later. But, when she reached the "Addio, del Passato" in Act III, her voice took on paler colors, and the effect was moving.

Under the direction of Herbert von Karajan, the Berlin Philharmonic and the Vienna Singverein (Helmuth Froschauer, director) offered Brahms' Requiem on Saturday evening, November 13 at Carnegie Hall. The soloists were baritone Jose Van Dam and soprano Leontyne Price.

By the end of the performance, one had the impression that one had heard something close to "definitive." In the solo "Ihr habt nun Traurigkeit," Miss Price floated her lovely lyric soprano exquisitely over the chorus and orchestra in a way that can only be described as magical.

Soprano Barbara Hendricks made her New York recital debut on Sunday afternoon, November 14 at Town Hall. With pianist Lawrence Skrobacs and clarinetist Richard Stoltzman, she offered works by Haydn, Fauré, Schubert, Matayas Seiber, Debussy, and Richard Strauss.

Miss Hendricks' artistry measures up to that of the best singers currently heard in this area. She has a bright, crystal clear voice in the Erna Berger tradition, but warmer. More important, however, is the fact that she has the rare ability to approach each work in a highly personal manner.[9]

33   High-Powered *Don Carlo*

A high-powered concert version of Verdi's opera *Don Carlo* climaxed the eleventh season of the Symphony of the New World on Sunday afternoon, August 4, 1976 at Carnegie Hall. Musical director Everett Lee was assisted by first-rate principals and Leo Warbington's New York Vocal Repertory Opera Chorus.

The cast included Esther Hinds as Queen Elizabeth, Olivia Stapp as Princess Eboli, Rolf Jupither as Rodrigo, Rolf Bjorling as Don Carlo, Simon Estes as King Philip II, McHenry Boatwright as the Grand Inquisitor, and Betty Lane as the Celestial Voice and other small roles.

With such fine artists, it came as no surprise that the quality of singing was on a very high level. The first show stopper was a fervently sung Act One duet by the two outstanding Swedish singers, Jupither and Bjorling. Like his father, Jussi, Bjorling has a secure top, but otherwise his voice is individual.

In the famous bass aria at the opening of Act Three, Estes poured out glorious tones in the grand manner, but always serving the text. And, although she pushed her voice to its limits, Ms. Stapp brought down the house with "O Don Fatale." The orchestra provided accompaniments which accented the drama.

The star of the afternoon was soprano Esther Hinds. She possesses, without question, one of the most ravishingly beautiful lyric-spinto voices on the American stage today. She brought out every expressive nuance in her aria "Tu che le vanita" and she moved us deeply.

Boatwright and Lane offered some fine singing in smaller roles and the choral passages were well done. Maestro Lee might have demanded from his forces a little more variety in dynamic color, but one could hardly wish for more dramatic excitement.[10]

Shortly after her appearance in this concert version of *Don Carlos,* Miss Hinds scored a personal success as Bess in the recent Houston Grand Opera production of *Porgy and Bess.* This was topped by a contract to sing the next season at the Metropolitan Opera.

Simon Estes, who in 1966 took a prize in the First International Tchaikowsky Vocal Competition in Moscow, has been appearing in major opera houses around the world. His first *Boris Godunov* in Lubeck, Germany, in 1974 was greeted with twenty-nine curtain calls.

McHenry Boatwright created a sensation in the leading role in Gunther Schuller's opera *The Visitation* with the Hamburg State Opera in 1966. He also took the same role in the first New York presentation of the opera (by the Hamburg company) in 1967 in the Metropolitan Opera House.

III

OPERAS AND OPERA COMPANIES

34 Operas by Black Composers

The highly publicized productions of Scott Joplin's opera *Treemonisha* have aroused interest in Black excursions in the world of lyric theater. As far as I can ascertain, the earliest efforts in this direction in the United States were those of H. Lawrence Freeman (1875–1954).

Although he wrote a total of fourteen operas, it was his *Voodoo*, produced in 1928 by the composer himself at The Palm Garden, that won the attention of New York critics. Freeman assembled a large cast and an all-Black orchestra to perform his work on this important occasion.

According to the *New York Times*: "At the first crash of cymbals and brass, shrilling of reeds and scraping of strings, it was apparent that here was either almost unbelievable discord—a mad melange that would kill a master musician—or a thing in new forms and new rhythms."

The death of Shirley Graham (Mrs. W. E. B. DuBois) has been widely reported in the press, but little has been said of her contributions to music. Her opera *Tom-Tom* was premiered on June 30, 1932, before an audience of fifteen thousand in the Cleveland Stadium (Ohio).

Produced by Dr. Ernest Lert and Lawrence A. Higgins, no expense was spared to stage this new work in the grand manner. The great baritone Jules Bledsoe, then at the peak of his career, was brought in to play the lead, and the opening night audience included Mary Garden and Vicki Baum.

With characteristic generosity, Herbert Elwell, critic of the *Cleveland Plain Dealer*, wrote: "In its present state, it impressed this reviewer more from a musical than a theatrical point of view, as a grand idea not quite perfectly realized . . . there were moments which contain the nucleus of real beauty."

The principals were given much praise. Elwell wrote: "Topping the list was Jules Bledsoe, who, as the Voodoo Man or high priest of the savages, was most convincing. His enormous baritone rolled out like thunder at times and added a rich luster to the general vocal quality."

Charlotte Murray was "forceful and persuasive" and Hazel Mountain Walker's song "seemed to call forth centuries of sorrow." Luther King's "tenor voice was most pleasing." The principal dancer, Festus Fitzhugh, "helped convey the primitive impulses of the barbaric tribes."

The first opera by a Black composer to be produced by a major company was William Grant Still's *Troubled Island*, based on a libretto by Langston Hughes. It was premiered on March 31, 1949, by the New York City Opera in honor of its fifth anniversary.

Based on the life of the Haitian leader Jean Jacques Dessalines, who ruled the country from 1803–1806, the libretto deals with subject matter above the usual operatic standard. And, it was fashioned from a successful play by the noted American poet Langston Hughes.

The opening night cast, under the baton of Laszlo Halasz,

included Robert Weede, Marie Powers, and Helena Bliss, all playing Black characters. It was staged by Eugene Bryden with scenery by H. A. Condell and ballets choreographed by George Balanchine and Jean Leon Destine.

Francis D. Perkins of the *New York Herald Tribune* said: "The music suggested that Mr. Still has a flair for opera, but one that is not fully developed; it also suggested intentions not yet fully realized in a musical idiom for this form . . . the composer's sincerity, however, was evident in the music."

Another opera based on the subject of Dessalines was Clarence Cameron White's *Ouanga* (libretto by John Frederick Matheus), which won the David Bispham Medal in 1933. Its first major New York performance was by the National Negro Opera Company in the Metropolitan Opera House on May 27, 1956.

In his review in the *New York Times*, Howard Taubman wrote: "The book is straightforward enough, and Mr. White has provided music of considerable seriousness and sweetness. But the tension and violence that the subject needs are not there."

Then there is *Treemonisha*. The title character is a pretty young thing from an Arkansas plantation dressed in calico, quite happy among her own people. Along came a white lady who took the opera to Atlanta, to Virginia, and to New York, where she was introduced to fast society. And Treemonisha was "ruint."

Like Vera Brodsky Lawrence, I first encountered the piano-vocal score of Scott Joplin's opera gathering dust on the library shelf. She went a step further and managed to get it produced by the music department of Morehouse College (Atlanta University) with the Atlanta Symphony on January 28 and 29, 1972.

The production started with a brilliant new orchestration by Black composer T. J. Anderson. A gifted cast, mostly well-known professionals, prepared the score under the musical direction of Wendell Whalum. Katherine Dunham was stage director and choreographer, and Robert Shaw was the conductor.

Time magazine reported: "Last week, at Atlanta's Memorial Arts Center, *Treemonisha* finally made it to the stage. It turned out to be of far more than historical interest. Despite its naïveté, the opera brims with jubilant rhythms and haunting melodies."

The *New York Times* critic wrote: "The audience tonight went out of its mind after hearing 'A Real Slow Drag.' There were yells, and great smiles of happiness, and curtain call after curtain call. If the rest of the opera were as breathtaking as this . . . the opera would run forever on Broadway."

Some rich white folks down at The Wolf Trap Foundation for the Performing Arts decided to invite Treemonisha to Virginia for a spell in the summer of 1972. They dressed her up in a brand new gown (orchestration by white William Bolcom), much to the surprise of her Black friends.

Then the Houston Grand Opera got her up bigger and better in true Texas fashion, and brought her to the Uris Theatre in New York on October 21, 1975. Among her companions were white orchestrator Gunther Schuller and white director Frank Corsaro, with Black choreographer Louis Johnson tagging along.

The Black folks have been talking about it ever since. They said that hussy went and sold out to the white folks and turned her back on her own—I mean T. J. Anderson, Katherine Dunham, and Wendell Whalum. They want to know if Treemonisha was the victim of the classic ripoff.

35   The Met's New *Aida*

On the surface, the announcement by the Metropolitan Opera that it was offering a new production of Verdi's *Aida* in the spring of 1976 did not strike me as being particularly significant. It had long been one of the most popular operas in the repertory, and many "new" productions had come and gone.

Based on the second performance on Saturday evening, February 7, however, this staging was the way the new regime announced with clarion tones that our opera house was working toward a performing style of its own. We have had some "stylish" productions before, but no genuine "house" style.

The basic concept was to show in sharp contrast the life styles of the Egyptians and the Ethiopians. The former were shown as trapped by the belief that royalty were gods and the latter as being genuine feeling human beings. Concept never got in the way of opera's core—great singing.

With one exception, the cast was completely American. It included Leontyne Price as Aida, James McCracken as Radames, Marilyn Horne as Amneris, James Morris as the king, Cornell MacNeil as Amonasro, Bonaldo Giaiotti as Ramfis, Charles Anthony as a messenger, and Marcia Baldwin as a priestess.

For the most part, the singing was uniformly fine, especially in the ensembles. Of course, Miss Price, who is the definitive Aida of our generation, dominated the performance. She was in excellent voice on this occasion and was rewarded with several ovations.

Special mention should go to Louis Johnson, whose dances were handled with wit and skill. The Act II, Scene 2 ballet in which the Egyptian soldier beats the Ethiopian through unfair means was superb. The excellent dancers were William Badolato and Stanley Perryman.

We will need more time to get used to the new settings, which were utilitarian by necessity, but properly suggestive of ancient Egypt. There could have been a little more light on stage, if for no better reason than to let the audience see the facial expressions of the singers more clearly.

Since this new production was a collaboration, thanks should go to James Levine as musical director, John Dexter as stage director, David Reppa as set designer, Peter J. Hall as costume designer, and Gilbert Hemsley as lighting designer and to the Gramma Fisher Foundation for its financial support.[1]

In reading through the program for this production of *Aida*, I was struck by an advertisement by RCA for its latest recording featuring Leontyne Price in the title role. It quotes the *Corriere della Sera* (Milan) as saying that "Our Verdi would have found her the ideal Aida."

This may very well be true. In his time, the idea of a Black singer in the role was remote. As far as I have been able to ascertain, the first was soprano Florence Cole-Talbert, who sang Aida in March of 1927 at the Teatro Comunale in Cosenza, Italy, with considerable success.

The *Calabria Fascista* reported that "her beautiful voice and expressive acting won her hearty applause from the large audience." It is interesting to note that Mme. Cole-Talbert became the first of her race to become a member of the Fascista Group of Lyric Artists.

The first Black singer to essay Aida with a major company in the United States was Caterina Jarboro on July 22, 1933, with Alfredo Salmaggi's Chicago Opera Company at the Hippodrome in New York City. A capacity audience studded with celebrities received her performance with wild enthusiasm.

She was cited by the *New York Times* for her "vivid dramatic sense" and "an Italian diction remarkably pure and distinct, a musicianly feeling for phrase and line, and a voice whose characteristically racial timbre, husky and darkly rich, endowed the music with an individual effectiveness."

Ellabelle Davis made her debut in the role on July 23, 1946, at the Opera Nacional in Mexico City. She attracted a brilliant first night audience that included President Romulo Betancourt of Venezuela, United States Ambassador Walter Thurston, and leaders of Mexican society.

According to the *New York Times*, "By the end of the first act her musical command of the role and her lovely voice were unquestionable to everyone, and her third act solo outside the Temple of Isis. 'O Patria Mia,' was in itself enough to make Miss Davis consider her debut a fine success."

The first Black Aida to appear at the Metropolitan Opera was the Brooklyn-born soprano Gloria Davy. Her appearance in the role on February 12, 1958, was also the occasion of her debut with the company. It began a career that lasted for several seasons.

The *New York Herald Tribune* found her "promising from a vocal point of view and unusually notable from a visual standpoint." The *New York Times* praised her "for beautiful phrasing, and her voice is a supple, free-flowing soprano that is clear and pure and yet also velvety and warm."

Since that time, many notable Black artists have sung Aida both here and abroad with great success. But it is Leontyne Price who will go down in operatic history as the definitive Aida of our generation. Yes, Giuseppe Verdi would have found her the ideal Aida.

36   Verdi's Chocolate Scheme

During the course of his long and illustrious career as an operatic composer, Giuseppe Verdi concerned himself with two major Black characters—Aida and Otello. *Otello* was presented here by Theatre National de l'Opera of Paris as part of its first American visit at the Metropolitan Opera House.

In a letter to his publisher Ricordi (August, 1879), Verdi referred to *Otello* as "the chocolate scheme" and complained about being manipulated into turning Shakespeare's drama into an opera. It was not until 1887 that the score was ready for its La Scala premiere.

One key to his attitude toward the central character is found in an August 15, 1880, letter to Boito, the excellent librettist: "After Otello has insulted Desdemona, there is nothing more to say—at the most a phrase, a reproach, a curse on the *barbarian* who has insulted a woman!"

Verdi was obviously more fascinated by the character of Iago, whom he visualized as "a tall, thin man with a receding forehead and narrow-set eyes, nonchalant and perfunctory in manner." He emerges as a many-faceted personality, while Otello is two-dimensional.

In the Paris Opera performance, on Wednesday, September 15, 1976, Carlo Cossutta sang Otello's opening "Esultate" with uncommon brilliance. As the opera progressed, the humanity of the character came through, achieved more through vocal than through physical means. But it was no mere stereotype.

Margaret Price is without question one of the great Desdemonas of our time. Her rich, seamless voice reached its peak in the final scene, which was magnificently sung. The effectiveness of the scene was enhanced by the presence of Jane Berbie in the role of Emilia.

In spite of some pitch problems and a general lack of focus in his voice, Gabriel Bacquier was masterful as the villainous Iago. He drew every nuance out of the "Credo" in Act II, and his business with the handkerchief in Act III was deftly handled.

The highly stylized concept of director Terry Hands did not obscure the music. There was a stark, Germanic setting by Joseph Svoboda and strangely incongruous costumes by Abd'el Kader Farrah. But Sir George Solti's solid musical direction placed Verdi's score center stage where it belonged.[2]

As far as I know, the only Black singer to essay the role of Otello was the tenor Laurence Watson. He appeared in a concert version of the opera with the Buffalo Philharmonic under William Steinberg on March 11, 1950. This event was broadcast on the NBC network.

This distinguished artist made a highly successful Town Hall recital debut on March 25, 1956, with Jonathan Brice at the piano. His program included two arias from *Otello*, "Tu? Indietro! Fuggi!" and "Niun mi tema." The *New York Times* reported that he "has a voice of power and brilliance."

37   The Saints Have Returned

In her book *Negro Musicians and Their Music*, (Washington, D.C.; Associated Music Publishers, Inc., 1936) Maude Cuney-Hare included Virgil Thomson with the Black composers without batting an eyelash. It is no secret that Thomson has always loved Black folks, and they have loved him well enough to make him an honorary member of the race.

One of the reasons for this mutual admiration is that his first opera, *Four Saints in Three Acts*, based on a text by Gertrude Stein, was so magnificently performed by an all-Black cast that it created a sensation both at its premiere in 1934 and in a revival in 1952.

The saints were with us again in multi-colored splendor (with an interracial cast) in the Forum at Lincoln Center during the spring of 1973. The opera had been revived by the Metropolitan Opera in a new series entitled Opera at the Forum, a kind of mini-Met in the tradition of the Piccola Scala.

Although this new production was prepared under the watchful eye of the composer, Alvin Ailey managed to add a few individual touches. But since he was not given a free hand to restage the work, the final result was something that was "half inside and half outside."

Each time I witness a revival of this opera, I marvel at the wit and charm of Thomson's score and at his skill at setting our language to music. If we ever get a permanent repertory company devoted to works of American lyric theater, this opera will be a staple.

Dominating the stage in the current production were Betty Allen and Benjamin Matthews as the Commere and Compere. There was also some fine singing by Clamma Dale (St. Therese I), Hilda Harris (St. Therese II), Arthur Thompson (St. Ignatius Loyola), Barbara Hendricks (St. Settlement), and Henry Price (St. Chavez).

Anyone who had ever seen photographs of the original settings and costumes would have been very disappointed with the ones by Ming Cho Lee and Jane Greenwood, respectively. But as Gertrude Stein remarked in *The Autobiography of Alice B. Toklas*, it is "a completely interesting opera both as to words and music." [3]

A brilliant audience, a most knowing one—an audience indeed, that included all our choicest spirits of modern verse, music and drama—gathered last night in the Forty-fourth Street Theatre and applauded itself hoarse at the end of the first performance in this city of the opera, *Four Saints in Three Acts*, the text by Gertrude Stein and the music by Virgil Thomson.

Thus began a review by Olin Downes in the February 20, 1934 edition of the *New York Times*. This production by John Houseman had choreography by Frederick Ashton, settings by Florine Stettheimer, and was conducted by Alexander Smallens. The cast included Edward Matthews as St. Ignatius, Beatrice Robinson Wayne as St. Theresa I, Bruce Howard as St. Theresa II, Altonell Hines as Commere, Abner Dorsey as Compere, and Leonard Franklyn as St. Chavez.

It was revived in 1952 at the Broadway Theatre, with artistic and musical direction by Thomson, associate conductor and choral director William Jonson, scenery and costumes by Paul Morrison based on designs by Florine Stettheimer, choreography by William Dollar, and book direction by Maurice Grosser.

The cast included Edward Matthews as St. Ignatius, Inez Matthews as St. Theresa I, Betty Lou Allen as St. Theresa II, Altonell Hines as Commere, Elwood Smith as Compere, and Rawn Spearman as St. Chavez. In the cameo role of St. Cecelia was Leontyne Price. This production was taken to Paris as the final offering of the International Exposition of "Masterpieces of the Twentieth Century."

38   *Porgy and Bess* Revisited

George Gershwin's opera *Porgy and Bess* has been with us for over forty years. But New York had to wait until Saturday evening September 25, 1976, to hear the score in its entirety when Sherwin M. Goldman and the Houston Grand Opera brought their production to the Uris Theatre for a limited run.

Throughout its history, *Porgy and Bess* has never gained the support of Black audiences to any large degree. When it first came on the scene in 1935, Blacks who had any interest in the arts were struggling to join the mainstream of American life. They did not care to remember Catfish Row.

Duke Ellington said: "The times are here to debunk Gershwin's lampblack Negroisms." Dr. Hall Johnson pointed out: "Mr. Gershwin's much-publicized visits to Charleston for local color do not amount even to a matriculation in the preparatory school that is needed for this work."

The Houston company was made up of artists who are too young to remember life in Catfish Row or the social conditions in 1935. They took the enlightened view that the inhabitants of the Row are no more authentic than Bizet's gypsies in *Carmen* or Mascagni's Sicilians in *Cavalleria*.

This company concerned itself with such artistic matters as how to handle the difficult transition in Act II, Scene 1, where Jake speaks of the necessity of earning a living to be answered suddenly by Porgy's "I've Got Plenty of Nothin'." A solution was found and an awkward moment was avoided.

When *Porgy and Bess* first came to light, there were very few Black singers with the kind of operatic experience necessary to cope with the score. Now Black singers are in every major opera company in the world and they can handle anything from Monteverdi to Ginastera.

In the Houston production, Donnie Ray Albert played the role of Porgy. He has a big powerful voice of considerable richness which he used to emphasize the toughness of Porgy's character rather than its lyrical side. This was valid, but it lacked the poetry of others who have played the role.

Clamma Dale's Bess reminded me of those marvelous "Negro" drawings of the Mexican painter Miguel Covarrubias. It was a little too urban, but a brilliant conception. Since her recital debut, she used her exquisite voice with much greater freedom.

The supporting cast was excellent. Betty Lane (Clara) sang "Summertime" poignantly; Wilma Shakesnider (Serena) sang her aria impressively; Larry Marshall (Sportin' Life) was evil and cunning; Andrew Smith (Crown) sang and acted well; Carol Brice (Maria) was superb; and Curtis Dickson (Jake) was fine.

Like the chorus in every production of *Porgy and Bess* I have ever heard, this one was absolutely first class. One had the feeling that within its ranks were any number of singers who could step into a principal role and do a fine job.

The settings and lighting by Robert Randolph and Gilbert V. Hemseley, Jr., respectively, were impressive. Nancy Potts's costumes were just fine. The overall production was stylishly directed by Jack O'Brien, and John De Main handled the musical direction with taste and authority.

I am still waiting to see *Porgy and Bess* in the opera house where it really belongs. It needs a larger orchestra to do full justice to the score. But, for now, I am quite satisfied with the Houston Grand Opera production, which has taken a giant step in that direction.[4]

When *Porgy and Bess* had its world premiere on October 10, 1935, at the Alvin Theatre in New York, criticism of the work far outweighed the praise. Olin Downes (The *New York Times*) found that Gershwin "has not completely formed his style as an opera composer. The style is at one moment of opera and another of operetta or sheer Broadway entertainment." It ran only 124 performances.

The cast is now legendary. It included: Todd Duncan as Porgy, Anne Wiggins Brown as Bess, Abbie Mitchell as Clara, Edward Matthews as Jake, John W. Bubbles as Sportin' Life, Ruby Elzy as Serena, Warren Coleman as Crown, and Georgette Harvey as Maria. The Eva Jessye Choir was also featured. Alexander Smallens was the musical director, and Rouben Mamoulian was in charge of staging.

Dr. Hall Johnson noted: "If these singing actors had been

as inexperienced as the composer, *Porgy and Bess* might have turned out to be as stiff and artificial in performance as it is on paper. Fortunately for all concerned, this is not the case. And I think it is a good show for no other reason than that it presents these capable people in an interesting and varied entertainment."

The magnificent artistry of these singers has been committed to the phonograph record. MCA (2035) has reissued the original Decca (DL7-9024) with Todd Duncan as Porgy and Anne Brown as Bess, Clara, and Serena. There is a special Mark 56 (641) disk of a rehearsal featuring the above artists and Abbie Mitchell and Ruby Elzy, with the composer conducting.

Since its premiere, *Porgy and Bess* has been revived many times with outstanding performers. It would take an entire volume to discuss them and, since so much has been written elsewhere, I shall forego that pleasure. However, I should like to bring to the reader's attention the essay "Porgy and Bess— A Folk Opera?" by Hall Johnson (*Opportunity*, 1936) and a book entitled *The Muses Are Heard* by Truman Capote (New York: Random House, 1956).

39 *Carmen* Moves "Down Home"

I was not present on that fateful day when Carmen moved (to borrow a term from Black parlance) "down home." On December 2, 1943, Oscar Hammerstein II and Robert Russell Bennett dressed her up in calico, changed her name to *Carmen Jones* and brought her to the Broadway Theatre.

Up to that time, New York had only seen *Carmen* in her grand opera guise, her "glad rags." I am referring to the sung recitatives interpolated by the American-born composer Ernest Guiraud (1837–1892). The subtleties of her charm had long been lost in the vast expanses of the Metropolitan Opera House.

Keeping in mind that Bizet originally conceived *Carmen* as an *opera comique*, Hammerstein and Bennett scaled down their production to the proportions of the legitimate theater and allowed their sun-tanned heroine to whisper and coo. When she cried out or shouted, the effect was powerful.

In all other respects, however, Hammerstein and Bennett departed from the original radically. They changed the locale from Spain to the American South. In this version, Carmen works in a factory that manufactures parachutes instead of cigarettes.

The real stroke of genius was the idea of casting the opera entirely with Black singing actors. In the *New York Herald Tribune*, Virgil Thomson commented: "Musically they have rhythm, real resonance, excellent pitch, perfect enunciation and full understanding of operatic convention."

Under the baton of Joseph Littau, the opening night principals included Muriel Smith as Carmen, Luther Saxon as Joe (Don Jose), Carlotta Franzell as Cindy Lou (Micaela), Glenn Bryant as Husky Miller (Escamillo), and June Hawkins as Frankie (Frasquita).

The chorus was trained by Robert Shaw. In the *Daily News*, John Chapman enthused, "The choruses, as one might guess because they are Negro voices, are superb—better than any I ever heard at the Met." This sentiment was echoed in all of the reviews.

Apparently the stage direction by Hassard Short was first-rate, as was the choreography for the ballet sequences by Eugene Loring. The costumes and settings by Raoul Pene DuBois and Howard Bay, respectively, were cited by *P.M.*'s critic Louis Kronenberger as "good and colorful."

In the title role, Miss Smith was careful not to fall into the trap of modeling her portrayal on the Met's reigning Carmens, Gladys Swarthout and Rise Stevens. One review said, "She is everything that is Carmen: beautiful, lithe, tempestuous, playful, dangerous, sultry, irresistible, coarse, fiery."

As Joe (Don Jose), Luther Saxon was "a splendid acting foil for Carmen, but he sings Joe perhaps a little too stiffly to match the free style of the others." Kronenberger (*P.M.*) spoke of his "quiet sincerity," while Henry Simon (also of *P.M.*) praised his "pleasant lyric tenor."

In the tradition of almost every singing actress who has essayed Micaela (in this case Cindy Lou), Carlotta Franzell stopped the show with her one aria. One critic noted: "Miss Franzell, an absolute newcomer to any stage, sings and acts like a great lady of the theater."

Glenn Bryant as Husky Miller (Escamillo) was "big, dominant and quite wonderful" (Kronenberger), and June Hawkins as Frankie (Frasquita) scored a big hit with an aria borrowed from Carmen. Simon (*P.M.*) said that she provided "the best vocalism of the evening."

As could be expected, some observers complained about the crudeness of Hammerstein's use of dialect. Because all of the singers were highly trained classical artists, they were able to handle the lyrics in such a way that they came through with remarkable authenticity.

Producer Billy Rose hired several outstanding singers as alternates for the principal roles so that their voices would remain fresh throughout the run. These included Muriel Rahn as Carmen, Napoleon Reed as Joe, and Elton J. Warren as Cindy Lou. Black conductor Everett Lee also joined the company.

Theater-goers filled the Broadway Theatre for a total of 231 performances. The excellent original-cast recording has been re-released by MCA (Decca: DL 79021).

One is always curious as to what happens to artists who come into celebrity as a result of a Broadway show such as *Carmen Jones.* They frequently receive rave notices laced with predictions of great things to come. And we wait eagerly to applaud their efforts again.

Miss Smith polished up her French and took a brief operatic journey to the Spanish setting when Alfredo Salmaggi presented her in the original *Carmen* at New York's Triboro Stadium. Of her portrayal critic Robert A. Hague wrote: "She acts the role with considerable grace and charm."

After a brief stint in the City Center Symphony production of *The Cradle Will Rock* by Marc Blitzstein, she made her formal recital debut on December 12, 1947, at Town Hall. With Stuart Ross at the piano, she sang a program that included works by Bach, Beethoven, and Hugo Wolf.

The *New York Herald Tribune* critic reported: "Miss Smith has a beautiful voice. It is resonant in all its ranges, and in its lowest register, as an instrument depicting gloom and despair, it is nothing short of astonishing . . . her interpretations never want in fire or temperament."

Miss Smith moved to London where she became a part of the musical scene. After becoming active in Moral Rearmament, she made a film on the life of Mary McCloud Bethune. She returned to New York for a revival in 1956 of *Carmen Jones* at City Center and then disappeared from the stage.

❋   ❋   ❋

Luther Saxon made his concert debut on May 26, 1946, at Times Hall before a large and enthusiastic audience. One critic wrote: "Mr Saxon's light tenor voice has a smooth and velvet-like quality that lends itself to a sort of miniature singing both attractive in itself."

A later recital at Town Hall drew the attention of the important vocal critic Noel Strauss. He noted that "the serious young vocalist could be commended for his musicality, his careful phrasing and clean-cut diction." Saxon, however, never went on to a major career.

After *Carmen Jones*, Carlotta Franzell returned home to Michigan, where she remained active for a long time. This was our loss, because she might have fulfilled the prediction of the *Herald Tribune* critic that "in time she may be a great coloratura soprano."

This comment referred to her pre-*Carmen* recital on November 18, 1942, at Town Hall. The reviewer also praised her singing of a Mozart aria by saying "the singer showed her ability to reach altissimo F's well within the vocal line and to impart a caressing vocal quality to the text."

40 Opera as Ballet

"Operatic masterpieces, like great cathedrals, are almost indestructible. They have weathered the storms of many a mediocre production by stage directors as well as numerous well-meaning attempts by dance choreographers to turn them into ballet."

Thus began my review of two attempts to turn opera (or operetta) into ballet. One of these was Alberto Alonzo's production of *Carmen* for the American Ballet Theatre, and the other was the Robert Helpmann–Ronald Hynd version of *The Merry Widow* for the Australian Ballet.

In rereading my article, the pages of time raced back to Wednesday evening, May 16, 1956, when the Black choreographer Anthony Basse presented a program entitled "Experiments in Choreographed Ballet" at the Countee Cullen Branch of the New York Public Library.

The operas were Mozart's one-act *Bastien and Bastienne* and Monteverdi's *Il Combattimento*. The dancers included Basse, Reggie Reid, and Betty Ann Thompson. The singers were Raoul Abdul, Billie Lynn Daniels, Robert Henson, and Charles Saunders. Brooks Alexander was the musical director.

More interesting of the two was the unique staging of the Monteverdi. This marvelous little music drama lent itself perfectly to ballet treatment. The narrator tells the story of the battle between Tancredi and Clorinda while they act it out. They have only a few lines to sing.

In Basse's concept, there was both a singing and a dancing Tancredi and Clorinda. While the dancing pair took center stage, the singing couple sat on a bench to the side. The narrator, who played a major role in the proceedings, was placed on the opposite side lit by a small spotlight.

Basically the same format was used for the Mozart. In this work, the singers were placed near the piano unseen, while the dancers enacted the story in the manner of the Salzburg marionettes. The results were a little less satisfactory than in the Monteverdi.

Anthony Basse has gone on to become Mme. Tamara Karpova, the Black Rhinestone of the Russian ballet, in that delightful company called Les Ballets Trocadero de Monte Carlo. But serious observers of the dance will always remember his early experiments in choreographed ballet.[5]

41   Black Opera Companies

Opera is a natural form of expression for Black singers. The idea of human passion being expressed in song requires absolutely no special adjustment for a Black audience. It responds to sung dialogue (recitative) as easily as it does to the spoken word.

This phenomenon can be understood best when one observes the traditional Holy Week sermon in a small unorthodox Black church. Here, the minister tells the story of the Crucifixion, half chanting, half speaking. When the emotional pitch rises almost to the breaking point, pure song emerges.

> Dey crucified my Lord,
> An' He never said a mumberlin' word.
> Dey crucified my Lord,
> An' He never said a mumberlin' word.
> Not a word, not a word,
> Not a word.

To find an equally poignant moment in music, one has to turn to Monteverdi, one of the greatest operatic composers the world has ever known. This deeply moving cry of despair finds a spiritual twin in Ariadne's famous lament from the opera *Arianna*, written in 1608.

> *Lasciatemi morire,*
> *Lasciatemi morire!*
> *E chi volete che mi conforte*
> *In cosi dura sorte,*
> *In cosi gran martire?*
> *Lasciatemi morire,*
> *Lasciatemi morire!*

Given this kind of musical tradition, it is not at all surprising that Blacks should excel in opera or lyric theater, depending on which designation one prefers. Because they were not accepted in the mainstream, the early Black opera singers had to start their own companies.

As early as 1873, a group of amateurs in Washington, D.C., founded the Colored American Opera Company. Under the musical direction of John Esputa, the company decided to present a number of performances of Julius Eichberg's *The Doctor of Alcantara*. Eichberg was the distinguished violinist-composer who founded the Boston Conservatory of Music. Born in Düsseldorf and educated at the Brussels Conservatory of Music, Eichberg (1824–1893) first taught in New York City before he settled down in Boston.

The first performances took place in Lincoln Hall on February 3rd and 4th. The *Daily Washington Chronicle* reported: "Lincoln Hall was literally packed. Of course the majority of the audience was colored and included a host of the personal friends of the singers."

In its review, the *Daily National Republican* had this to say: "Under all the circumstances, they sing and perform extraordinarily well; and as for the chorus, it is superior to that of any German or Italian opera heard in this city for years."

The company gave three performances in Philadelphia on February 21, 22, and 23 in Agricultural Hall. The *Philadelphia Evening Bulletin* said: "The opera was given in a really admirable manner by singers who understand their business and have vocal gifts of no mean description."

The *Philadelphia Inquirer* observed: "The chorus, composed of probably thirty voices, male and female, was a feature; and their singing is really unsurpassed by the finest chorus in the best companies." This was a sentiment echoed in reviews of Black operatic performances up to the present day.

When the history of Blacks in opera is written, the names of these pioneers should be remembered: Agnes Gray Smallwood, Lena Miller, Mary Coackley, Henry F. Grant, Richard Tompkins, William T. Benjamin, George Jackson, and Thomas H. Williams. Henry Donohoe was business manager for each of them.

It was not until 1900, when Theodore Drury organized the Drury Grand Opera Company, that Blacks were seen in the standard European operatic repertory. He wisely chose to give only one opera each season at the beginning, each sung in English translation.

According to an article from the *Colored American* and reprinted in the *Negro Music Journal* (January 1903), the early productions had been *Carmen, Il Guarany*, and *Faust. Il Guarany*, which had its premiere at La Scala, was by the Brazilian Mulatto composer Antonio Carlo Gomez (1836–1896).

It was inevitable that the company should turn its attention to Verdi's *Aida*. With an orchestra conducted by Dr. Felix Jaeger, the performance took place on May 11, 1903, at the

Lexington Opera House (Terrace Garden), which was located on Fifty-eighth Street near Third Avenue.

For this, Drury chose a steller cast that included Estelle Clough as Aida, Alfrida Wagner as Amneris, George L. Ruffin as Amonasro, David Manser as Ramfis, Francis Van Arsdalen as the king, Oliver Taylor as the messenger, and Drury himself as Radames.

The *Colored American* was enthusiastic in its praise. Of Miss Clough it said "she won enthusiastic applause and sang with artistic feeling." Drury "was in fine voice and sang 'Celestial Aida' with excellent coloring and vividness." Ruffin "added splendid effort to the company."

Apparently this performance was not only the artistic but also the social event of the season. The review noted that "After the opera, dancing was indulged in until 4 A.M. The affair is pronounced a marked success, as regards office receipts as well as social patronage."

The success of the first production of *Aida* led to a revival on May 28, 1906, at the 14th Street Theatre. According to the *New York Times* (May 29): "It was noticed that the maidens chosen to represent Ethiopians were light in color while those representing Egyptians were darker as a rule."

Again Miss Clough played the leading role. The *Times* noted: "She remembered at all times that she was a King's daughter although in captivity and in sweeping across the stage, had a royal gait. Frequently she won applause with her high notes."

Alternating in the title role was Daisy Allen. The rest of the principals were James Wortham as Radames, Genevieve Motley as Amneris, Drury as Amonasro, and George Taylor as the king. Drury, according to the *Times*, "made a figure that aroused the deep sympathy of the audience."

The review also noted that "A good part of the audience was colored too and the boxes were filled by the leaders of New York's colored society. In the rear of the house there was a large gathering of serious-faced Negro men who were dressed in the height of fashion."

An editorial in an unidentified newspaper announced that Drury acquired ground on which to build an opera house for Blacks. Stocks were offered at $100 per share. Although the project did not materialize, he continued to provide a show-case for Black operatic talent for many years to come.

According to a brochure circulated in the summer of 1934, a new opera company was founded by Peter Creatore, who announced that "the primary object of The Aeolian Opera Association is to lend a helping hand to the Negro artist by making it possible for him to demonstrate his ability."

Its first season was to take place in Mecca Auditorium (now City Center). Among the operas scheduled were: Gruenberg's *The Emperor Jones* (June 29); *Cavalleria Rusticana* (July 11); *Rigoletto* (August 8); *Lakme* (August 22); and *Carmen* (August 29).

The brochure listed members of the company and the list was most impressive indeed. Included were such names as Jules Bledsoe, Anne Wiggins Brown, Minto Cato, Carl Diton, R. Todd Duncan, Ruby Elzy, Taylor Gordon, Abbie Mitchell, Charlotte Murray, Edith Sewell, and Laurence Watson.

After many delays, the season finally opened on July 10th with a double bill of *The Emperor Jones* and *Cavalleria Rusticana*. A front-page story in *Negro World* heralded it as "One of the most important steps in the progress of the Negro race. . . ."

Of Bledsoe's performance in *Emperor*, Peter Sanborn of

the *World-Telegram* wrote: "Here was a primitive magnificence of sheer power which is of exceeding rarity whether in the drama that is spoken or is sung. And it was projected largely through the native splendor of Mr. Bledsoe's voice."

Sanborn was also impressed with *Cavalleria.* He said that Abbie Mitchell as Santuzza "acted intelligently and sang with skill and artistic feeling." And, of R. Todd Duncan's performance as Alfio, he wrote that he (Duncan) "disclosed a strong and ringing baritone voice."

Unfortunately the public did not rush to the box office, and the company folded immediately. A headline in the *Afro-American* dated July 21, 1934, summed it up briefly: "N.Y. NOT READY FOR COLORED OPERA, HARLEM GROWS COLD, LEAVES BROADWAY HOLDING THE BAG."

Perhaps the most remarkable character in the chronicle of Black opera companies was Mary Cardwell Dawson, founder, president, and general manager of the National Negro Opera Company. For two decades beginning in 1941, she carried forward almost single-handedly the banner of Black opera.

Born in North Carolina and trained at the New England Conservatory of Music and the Chicago Musical College, she was successively soprano, teacher, conductor, and impresario. Her first venture was the Cardwell School of Music in Pittsburgh, which she operated from 1927 until 1941.

She also organized the Cardwell Dawson Choir, which performed at the World Fairs of Chicago in 1933 and New York in 1939. It toured nationally and won many prizes. She was the first woman to become president of the National Association of Negro Musicians.

Her production of *Aida* at the N.A.N.M. convention in Pittsburgh in 1941 led directly to the founding of the National Negro Opera Company. Its first production, also *Aida,* was presented on October 30, 1941, at the Syrian Mosque in Pittsburgh and repeated at the Chicago Civic Opera House in 1942.

La Rhea Julia sang the title role on both occasions, with William Franklin in Pittsburgh and Napoleon Reed in Chicago as Radames. In the many productions of this opera over the years, the title role was sung by Minto Cato, Muriel Rahn, Gertrude Overstreet, and Omega King.

Mrs. Dawson's most spectacular success was *La Traviata* at the Water Gate in Washington, D.C., which was witnessed by fifteen thousand people on August 28, 1943. Critics and public were impressed with the performances of Lillian Evanti as Violetta, Joseph Lipscomb as Alfredo, and Charles Coleman as Germont.

The chorus of one hundred was described by one major critic as "by far the best vocally and dramatically that has been heard in opera performances in this city." Another said that "the professional standards of the Metropolitan and Chicago Opera were surpassed."

This production went on to Pittsburgh, Chicago, and Madison Square Garden in New York, where it played to a crowd of twelve thousand. The cast included Mme. Evanti, Minto Cato, Lillian M. Smith, Joseph Lipscomb, William Franklin, Oscar Griffin, Edward Boatner, Wilson Woodbeck, and Horace Wilson.

The National Negro Opera Company never had enough money. Each year the company virtually died and each year, through Mrs. Dawson's indefatigable efforts, it was born again. In fact, there are many amusing stories told among musicians about the company's financial troubles.

At the famous Water Gate performance, the curtain almost didn't go up. Mme. Evanti refused to perform until she was paid. While fifteen thousand people waited, Mrs. Dawson had to raise Evanti's fee on the spot, after which the diva slipped the money in her bosom and the curtain went up.

During a production of *Aida* featuring Muriel Rahn and Napoleon Reed, the orchestra simply stopped playing in the middle of the opera and demanded payment. Once, during a production of *Faust*, Todd Duncan came out on stage and handed Mrs. Dawson a blank check so that the performance could begin.

Mrs. Dawson's basic plan was to organize chapters or opera guilds in various cities with the hope that each would raise enough money to finance a local appearance of the company. These were founded in Pittsburgh, Chicago, Washington, and New York.

The climax of Mrs. Dawson's career came on May 27, 1956, when the National Negro Opera Company presented *Ouanga* by Clarence Cameron White at the Metropolitan Opera House. This was the first time that a company other than the Metropolitan itself had presented an opera there.

According to the *Herald Tribune*, McHenry Boatwright sang the role of Dessalines, emperor of Haiti, "with considerable persuasiveness and a good voice . . . Juanita King sang appealingly as Defilee, Adelaide Boatner very commendably as Mougali and Lisle Greenidge as the Papaloi."

For the first time in a National Negro Opera Company production, most of the orchestra was Black. Later that same year, on September 29th, a fully staged version of *Ouanga* was presented at Carnegie Hall. The cast was the same, with the exception of Carol Brice as Mougali.

By the time of her death in March of 1962, Mrs. Dawson's protégés were singing in the great opera houses of the world. Robert McFerrin was at the Metropolitan, Camilla Williams,

William Dupree, and Lawrence Winters at the New York City Opera and McHenry Boatwright at the Hamburg State Opera.

Nora Holt, one of the most respected Black music critics, once wrote in the *Amsterdam News*: "Mary Cardwell Dawson and her brainchild, the National Negro Opera Company, have done more to inspire the love of opera in our musicians and our Negro public than any other person or medium in history."

Unique in American musical history were the international operatic productions at Karamu Theatre in Cleveland, Ohio. For almost two decades, under the direction of Dr. Benno D. Frank, this semiprofessional group offered operas on a continuous run basis in the manner of spoken plays.

During the official opening week of the new theater unit in the fall of 1949, Karamu presented a double bill of Gian Carlo Menotti's *The Medium* and Stravinsky's *The Tale of a Soldier*. On opening night, a small chamber orchestra was used under the direction of Leonard Shure.

The opening night cast included Zelma George, the sociologist and musicologist, as Madam Flora; Gloria Whitley as Monica; Charles Bettis as the mute Toby; Beverly Dame, from the original Broadway cast, as Mrs. Gobineau; Charles King as Mr. Gobineau; and Gladys Tiff as Mrs. Nolan.

Due in great part to the magnificently terrifying performance by Mrs. George as Madam Flora, *The Medium* ran for sixty-seven performances and as a result she was invited by the composer to star in a Broadway revival of the opera in the summer of 1950, where it ran for one hundred and two performances.

In the smaller arena auditorium, the Karamu opera players offered the American premiere of Karl Orff's *The Wise*

Woman (*Die Kluge*). Among those in the cast were Charles King, Virginia Robinson, Sherman Sneed, Howard Roberts, Elizabeth Foster, and myself.

The creator of Karamu's opera wing, Dr. Benno D. Frank, was a product of the German stage—he once worked with the Schiller Theatre and other houses in Hamburg. His dream for Karamu was to create a professional lyric theater which would include a touring company.

The basic philosophy of Karamu at that time was to bring together people of different racial backgrounds to share an artistic experience on a community level. Unfortunately, Dr. Frank's idea of creating a professional lyric theater did not materialize.

However, he did maintain professional performance standards. He guided his singers through the American premieres of such works as Ernest Bloch's *Macbeth*, Benjamin Britten's *Let's Make an Opera*, Janacek's *Katya Kabanova*, and Gluck's comic opera *Pilgrims to Mecca*.

It was my good fortune to sing the role of Guglielmo in Mozart's *Cosi Fan Tutte* for seventeen of its twenty-four performances under Dr. Frank's direction. Helmut Wolfes was the marvelous musical coach. This was one of Karamu's few attempts at what is known as "standard" opera.

A short item appeared in the February 1, 1967, issue of the *Cleveland Press* announcing that "Dr. Benno Frank, veteran director of plays and musical productions at Karamu, sent his resignation to Karamu's board of directors." After his departure at the season's end, there was no more opera at Karamu.

Founded in 1971 by a crusading Catholic nun, Sister M. Elise, Opera-South in Jackson, Mississippi, is the most active

Black opera company on the current scene. It is sponsored by three largely Black colleges: Jackson State, Utica Junior, and Tougaloo.

Beginning with productions of *Aida* and *Turandot,* the company gradually moved into the direction of operas by Black composers. In November of 1971 they chose two one-acters, *The Juggler of Our Lady* by Ulysses Kay and *Highway No. 1, U.S.A.* by William Grant Still. With an orchestra of thirty-eight white musicians conducted by Margaret Harris, a steller cast gave fine performances of these two works. The Kay opera featured Mervin Wallace and the Still showcased the talents of Wilma Shakesnider, Clyde Walker, and William Brown.

One of the outstanding Opera-South productions was the world premiere of Still's *A Bayou Legend* in November of 1971. *Time* magazine said that it "revealed Still as a kind of American Grieg—a miniaturist gifted with melody, an unerring sense of color and a fondness for the folklore."

It was imaginatively staged by Donald Dorr, with Leonard De Paur as conductor. Among the principals were Barbara Conrad, Robert Mosley, Juanita Waller, John Miles, and Francois Clemmons. The *Clarion Ledger* reported that "the chorus always has been one of Opera-South's strongest points."

Opera-South operates on an annual budget of approximately $100,000. Its current general manager is Delores Ardoyno, who has recently told the press, "We hope in the future to commission operas from Black composers. At least, we can promise them a performance."

*   *   *

In New York, the Harlem Opera Society under the direction of Emory Taylor has been experimenting with jazz improvisational operas. Together with Sam Rivers, Taylor created *Solomon and Sheba*, which was premiered at Clark Center in June of 1973 with great success.

This group was founded in 1960 by Monte Norris, the nephew and foster son of Theodore Drury. Like the Drury Grand Opera Company, it started out by giving performances of standard operas. Its present director, Emory Taylor, has brought new excitement to the company with his innovative ideas.

Inspired by the success of Opera-South, a distinguished committee on the east coast founded National Opera Ebony in 1974. Its founders and directors included Sister M. Elise, Benjamin Matthews, Ernest George, Margaret Harris, Wayne Sanders, and Paul Freeman.

In his review of *Carmen Jones* in the December 5, 1943, edition of the *New York Herald Tribune*, Virgil Thomson called the composition "a contribution to the repertory of that permanent Negro opera company that is going to provide the solution one day for all our opera problems." But that permanent opera company has not yet come into being. When it does, I hope that it will be housed in a big, beautiful home of its own. In its lobby, I hope there will be a marble plaque filled with the names of all the pioneers who laid its spiritual foundation.

42   Opera Ebony Makes Its Bow

A capacity audience filled Philadelphia's Academy of Music on Thursday evening, April 1, 1976, when National Opera Ebony made an auspicious debut in an English-language production of Verdi's warhorse, *Aida*. It was masterfully held together by the distinguished conductor Everett Lee.

Founded in 1974 by an enterprising group of young people, the company is designed to provide opportunities for Blacks to become fully involved in operatic production. Its secondary purpose is to develop Black audiences for grand opera, a noble aim worthy of wide support.

The large, distinguished cast included Alpha Floyd as Aida, Mervin Wallace as Radames, Barbara Conrad as Amneris, Eugene Holmes as Amonasro, Benjamin Matthews as Ramfis, Earl Grandison as the king, Gregory Hopkins as the messenger, and Wilhelmina Fernandez as the high priestess.

For the most part, the singing and acting was on a very high level. Especially thrilling were the lovely, high pianissimi of the soprano voice of Miss Floyd; the driving, almost overwhelming mezzo of Miss Conrad; and, above all, the sonorous, ringing baritone of Holmes.

The staging by Louis Galterio was idiomatic and intelligent, but the strength of this production was in things musical. Maestro Lee managed to keep his large forces under tight control without inhibiting individual expression. And he never covered the singers, a rarity on the operatic stage these days.

As was to be expected, the choral work was outstanding, with the Philadelphia Community Singers (Clayton White, director) and the Byrne Camp Chorale combining forces. Under the guidance of Arthur Hall, the Afro-American Dance Ensemble provided ballet sequences which were done with youthful enthusiasm.

The noted critic Virgil Thomson once wrote that "Negro singers, as always, make opera credible . . . they never look bored or out of place on a stage or seem inappropriately cast for any musical style." This was certainly the case in this production of *Aida*.

Now for the famous critical "but . . ." At least this observer hopes that National Opera Ebony will now focus attention on works by Black composers and bring to its audiences these sadly neglected scores. It is time to stop revitalizing tired old European classics and turn to the now! [6]

IV

KEYBOARD ARTISTS

43   Hazel Harrison Remembered

One of the earliest Black concert pianists to have a major career was Hazel Harrison (1881–1969). Her early training was under the guidance of Victor Heinze in Chicago, after which she went to Germany to study with such masters as von Dalen, Busoni, and Petri.

In 1904, she appeared as soloist with the Berlin Philharmonic. *Die Post* reported: "The pianist is still very young, and her touch lacks physical strength yet, but her delivery revealed feeling and individuality and her technical certainty bespoke of thorough schooling."

When she returned to the United States, she began annual concert tours that took her all over the country. Besides playing recitals, she was engaged as soloist by major symphony orchestras in Chicago, Minneapolis, and Los Angeles. These appearances were met with great critical success.

Among the voluminous clippings in the special collection of the library at Atlanta University, I found a review of one of her Town Hall recitals on October 15, 1930. The *New York Times* wrote: "To this representative program the soloist brought a full and singing tone and deft pedaling."

Her programs were put together with considerable taste. Her early training with Busoni accounted for the heavy dose of his Bach transcriptions and pieces by Liszt. But she also played contemporary music by Stravinsky and Ravel, and she featured a number of Black composers.

I heard her play a recital at the Euclid Avenue Baptist Church in Cleveland on November 23, 1947. On that occasion, she played Liszt's *St. Francis Walking on the Waves*. I still have a picture in my mind's eye of this fine artist majestically presiding over the keyboard.

44   Philippa Schuyler at Carnegie Hall

At one time or another we have all gone into a museum and tried to cover the whole collection in one visit—and come away a bit dizzy. This is how I felt when I left Carnegie Hall on Sunday afternoon June 7, 1959 when pianist Philippa Duke Schuyler completed a recital under the auspices of the Church of the Master.

Unfortunately, her program was composed entirely of short pieces, many of which are what I call of "salon cut." Included was John Kelley's "Oriental Suite," Moussorgsky's *Pictures at an Exhibition*, Griffes' "Roman Sketches," and several popular items by Ravel and Chopin. There was little the listener could sink his teeth into.

Probably the most satisfying playing of the afternoon was

offered in the Moussorgsky, which seemed perfectly suited to Miss Schuyler's musical and imaginative resources. It was evident that she had a vivid image of each vignette in her mind's eye which she was able to project to the listener.

In the more demanding works that required technical polish such as Ravel's "Jeaux d'Eau" and "Alborada del Gracioso," I became painfully aware that Miss Schuyler's resources are not of the caliber expected of one with so much experience and celebrity.[1]

Although Philippa Duke Schuyler began playing at the age of four, it was not until she was fifteen that she made her first major New York appearance. On July 13, 1946, she played the Saint-Saens Piano Concerto in G Minor with the New York Philharmonic at Lewisohn Stadium before twelve thousand people.

The *New York Times* reported: "She revealed herself as a pianist, without regard to age, of extraordinary natural talent. Her grasp of the broad line of each of the three movements of the concerto was complete, and she disclosed imagination to be found only in artists of a high level."

Thus began a career that took her on many world tours. She also found time to compose. Her early orchestral piece "Rumpelstiltskin," written at the age of thirteen, was played at her Philharmonic debut. She wrote several books, the last being *Who Killed the Congo?* (New York: Devin-Adair Co., 1962).

In 1967, Miss Schuyler was killed in a United States Army helicopter in Da Nang Bay, South Vietnam, while trying to evacuate Roman Catholic school children to Da Nang. Two thousand people attended a requiem mass presided over by Cardinal Spellman at St. Patrick's Cathedral.

45   Miss Hinderas's Philharmonic Debut

The long-awaited debut of pianist Natalie Hinderas with the New York Philharmonic finally took place on Friday afternoon, November 24, 1972. Under the direction of Stanislaw Skrowaczewski, she appeared as soloist in the Concerto for Piano and Orchestra by Argentinian composer Alberto Ginastera.

Since her Town Hall recital here in 1954, Miss Hinderas has played an all-Ravel program as part of the Coffee Concerts series in Harlem and was soloist with the Symphony of the New World at Lincoln Center. These appearances all provided a musical hors d'oeuvre before the main course.

The Ginastera concerto is a monumental work in four movements, each divided into carefully organized but complex smaller sections. There are dazzling rhythmic effects and striking tonal colors. A master composer, he exploits every instrument to the maximum.

As was to be expected, the orchestra reveled in this challenge and played the score superbly. Miss Hinderas, who was inspired by her recent triumph with the Philadelphia Orchestra in this work, played with fire and brilliance. Not one phrase was played unmusically, a genuine miracle.

The Friday afternoon subscription audience is not known for its enthusiasm for new music, nor is it given to being demonstrative toward new artists. Therefore, it is noteworthy that it accorded Miss Hinderas a long ovation. I should like to think that a small part of it was for the concerto, too.[2]

"The internationally recognized foremost Black woman pianist has come to the conclusion that although the composers of music were color-blind, many impresarios, conductors and managers in the United States are biased when it comes to hiring Black artists."

This statement appeared in a feature article about Natalie Hinderas in the *Evening Star* (Washington, D.C.) on November 9, 1971. Miss Hinderas's own career is a testament to its validity. And she has been in the forefront of the campaign to expand opportunities for Black artists.

Miss Hinderas was one of the first Black pianists to be handled by a major management in the fifties—Columbia Artists. She made major appearances on NBC–TV network programs and a highly successful Town Hall debut. This was followed by a tour of the country and then a period of relative silence.

In 1972, she made a sensational debut with the Philadelphia Orchestra and the New York Philharmonic as soloist in Ginastera's Piano Concerto. The *New York Times* wrote: "The solo part is a blockbuster and it was brilliantly played by the deceptively diminutive pianist."

She is just beginning to get the opportunities she so richly deserves. Like the Black mother in Langston Hughes' poem "Mother to Son," she can truly say:

> I'se still climbin',
> And, life for me ain't been no crystal stair.

46   Andre Watts at Lincoln Center

Pianist Andre Watts returned to Avery Fisher Hall on Sunday afternoon, February 1, 1976, to play his ninth consecutive recital in the "Great Performers at Lincoln Center" series. As usual, the house was sold out in advance and additional seats had to be placed on stage.

The program was devoted to the works of two composers—Franz Schubert and George Gershwin. The former was represented by Twelve Valses Nobles (Opus 77), Sonata in A Major (Opus 120) and Three Impromptus (D. 946) and the latter by Three Preludes and a solo adaptation of the famous *Rhapsody in Blue.*

One can only marvel at the technical brilliance of Watts's playing, which seems to grow with each passing year. Mature artists like Rudolf Serkin bring out more of the expressive values in the Schubert sonata, but Watts's youthful impetuousness is refreshing.

In the Gershwin work, Watts played in what can only be described as "the grand manner." Sharp contrasts, dramatic rhythmic accents and a final big climax brought the audience to its feet in a standing ovation at the conclusion of the *Rhapsody*.

In the year of the Bicentennial, it might have been interesting if Watts had focused attention on the genuine Black piano works of R. Nathaniel Dett (1882–1943), William Grant Still (b. 1895), and John Work (1901–1968). But we had to settle for Gershwin's "ersatz" excursions into Black musical culture.[3]

"A keyboard athlete of undisputed superiority, he is now at the height of his muscular power and has, in addition, the right combination of looks, charm and hint of mystery to qualify as an ideal American hero." These lines, which recently appeared in the *New York Times*, refer to Andre Watts, who, at the age of sixteen, became the first Black instrumental soloist since the turn of the century to appear with the New York Philharmonic Orchestra.

Up to this time, the doors that led to the stages of major concert halls throughout the world were closed tight to the Black instrumentalist-soloist. Once in a while they were cracked open for just a fleeting moment to admit one of the handful of extraordinarily gifted artists to make an occasional appearance under the baton of some benevolent conductor. But in spite of what might have been a great success at that moment, no concert manager would risk the perils of trying to build a career for one of these artists. So, soon after the rare moment, stage doors would snap shut as tightly as before.

On January 31, 1963, a miracle occurred in the world of classical music. Sixteen-year-old Andre Watts, an unknown young Black pianist, walked out on the stage at Philharmonic Hall to play the Liszt E-flat Concerto with the New York Philharmonic Orchestra under Leonard Bernstein. As soon as the notes of the final cadenza sounded, the audience broke out into an ovation that lasted almost fifteen minutes. And the echoes of this applause resounded via the press throughout the world.

In the western edition of the *New York Times*, critic Ross Parmenter wrote, "After the opening display of power there came a ravishing modulation to poetic lyricism. The young man made the ensuing gentle passages sing exquisitely." Soon after, *Time* and *Newsweek* devoted columns heralding the coming of this new artist-hero. As if by magic, the doors to every major concert manager's office, as well as the previously unfriendly stage doors of symphony orchestras, were not only unlocked, but propped open.

In reality, it was not magic alone that created this moment. There was careful manipulation on the part of the shrewd, professional Leonard Bernstein, one of the most powerful figures on the American symphonic scene. Glenn Gould was originally scheduled to play with the orchestra, but he fell ill a few days before. Andre Watts had recently created a sensation on the nationally televised Young People's Concerts of the Philharmonic, and fan mail was flooding into the offices of CBS. Nevertheless, it took a lot of hard thinking before Bernstein could justify giving such an important assignment on the Philharmonic's regular subscription series to a youngster with so little performing experience.

In an interview after the concert, Bernstein said, "Normally, I would never do such a thing. After all, he's just a boy, just a high school boy. But he's not just another great young pianist. The point is that he's one of those special giants. The seeds of his gianthood are already there. So it seemed a shame not to give him a chance. He just walked right out there like a Persian prince and played it. One day he'll undoubtedly be one of a very special dozen of the world's top pianists."

Much to the credit of both his newly acquired manager and his mother, there was no great effort to cash in on Andre's sudden rise to fame at the risk of what could be a long-term career. After much deliberation, it was agreed that Andre would play only six concerts the first year, twelve the following, and fifteen the next. And he would record the Liszt Concerto for Columbia Records so that the world could share this great moment. No sooner had the ink dried on the contracts than the Wattses returned to Philadelphia. Andre had to go back to his academic and musical studies.

Born on June 20, 1947, in Nuremberg, Germany, Andre is the son of an Afro-American father and a Hungarian mother. His father, Sergeant Herman Watts, was stationed in Germany when he married Maria Alexandra Gusmits. With the exception of one year when his father was assigned to a post in Philadelphia, Andre spent his first eight years on army posts in Germany. His musical training began at the age of four, when he began to play a miniature violin. By the age of six, he showed a preference for the piano and began lessons with his mother, an accomplished pianist in her own right. He recalls, "Soon I knew I preferred the piano. I had the hands for it and I was more at home at the keyboard."

When Andre was eight, his father was transferred back to

the United States, and the family settled down in Philadelphia. He was enrolled in an academic school as well as in the city's famous Academy of Music. Besides keeping up with his regular school work, he managed to find time to practice the piano about four hours a day. His progress was so phenomenal that, by the time he was nine, he won a competition over forty other gifted youngsters. The prize was an engagement with the Philadelphia Orchestra at its Children's Concerts. This began a long and ardent love affair between the orchestra and Andre, which continues to this day.

During his school years in Philadelphia, Andre did not feel that he belonged to any particular race. He was regularly "called out" by his classmates and beaten up after school, but he insists that this was not because he was Black or played the piano. It simply happened to everybody. The Irish boys fought the Italian boys and the Black boys fought them both. He found a solution to the problem of this situation by teaching himself a little judo. Soon the beatings stopped.

Eventually Andre's parents divorced. Andre always respected his father and remembers him as "a damn good soldier" who always wore amazingly shiny shoes and had his own system of ethics. He believed that if a relationship came to an end, then it should be finished without regrets. It is in this spirit that Andre accepted his father's departure from the household. He hasn't heard from him since.

Andre and his mother moved into an unusual little three-story house with only one room to a floor and a winding staircase. Because of its peculiar structure, the all-important piano had to be placed on the first floor together with a narrow sofa bed on which Andre could sleep. To make sure that Andre could develop his talents fully, Mrs. Watts created an isolated little world around him. She did everything she could to supply her son with the emotional security so necessary in the life of an artist.

After he completed his studies in Philadelphia, Andre did advanced work with Leon Fleisher at the Peabody Conservatory, from which he eventually was graduated. At that time, Andre told one reporter, "Maintaining school and concerts during the season is a problem. I've tried to study on planes and in hotel rooms, but I like to concentrate on one thing at a time and cannot do both. So I've worked out my schedule so that I do five dates and come back to school work."

Of his work with Fleisher, Andre said, "The biggest tribute to him—and the most beautiful thing—is that when I first came to him, he told me what the position of a teacher is. He told me to bring him a piece of music and, with it, several possibilities and ideas for the music. 'The ideal way,' he said, 'is that you have your own ideas and then I give you mine. Then you can see them all in front of you and finally evolve your own way and your own manner in the end.' "

Before a pianist can consider himself a complete artist, he must prove himself in a solo recital. At this moment, he must walk out on a bare stage with only a piano, a spotlight, and the sum total of his own musical personality. The auditorium is filled with experts (critics and other pianists) and a discriminating public used to hearing the world's greatest artists. They are waiting to analyze every musical phrase. The pianist is, in the phrase beautifully coined by the *New York Times* feature writer Joan Barthel, "on the threshold of the big plunge."

For Andre, this moment came on October 26, 1966, at

Philharmonic Hall, where his New York debut recital was placed daringly within the framework of the Great Performers Series. Of this event Harold C. Schonberg, the chief critic of the *New York Times*, reported, "He has the power of communication and the audience loved what it heard. This kind of pianistic as opposed to musical authority is rare from one of Mr. Watts' years, even considering the general high level of piano playing today. May his artistry also develop in line with such a natural gift." Another distinguished critic, Winthrop Sargeant of the *New Yorker* magazine, found Andre "a bravura pianist whose style takes one back to the great days of men like Moriz Rosenthal."

Of the act of performing, Andre told one writer, "My greatest satisfaction is performing. The ego is a big part of it, but far from all. Performing is my way of being part of humanity—of sharing. I don't want to play for a few people, I want to play for thousands. . . . There's something beautiful about having an entire audience hanging on a single note. I'd rather have a standing ovation than have some chick come backstage and tell me how great I was. When people come around after a concert it's less pleasant, because they're trying to get a piece of me."

When Andre is not on tour, his day usually begins around 8:00 A.M. with yoga exercises, shower, and breakfast of orange juice, raw egg yolks, corn flakes, and coffee. He usually practices from nine or ten until noon with a break for lunch and a short nap. This is followed by more yoga and practice at the piano until seven in the evening. He usually eats dinner with his mother. He rarely goes out and dislikes parties, because they are "a great waste of life force." Instead, he spends his evenings chatting with a few friends or reading musical scores and books.

Over a period of ten short years, Andre has become what is known in the music business as "one of the hottest properties." This means he plays almost one hundred dates a year and commands a fee of about $6,000 per concert. He is booked around the world for three seasons ahead. One of the highlights of his career is that he was chosen to be the first American pianist to play in Red China—as soloist with the Philadelphia Orchestra.

47   Miss Cole Plays The Harpsichord

After harpsichordist Frances Cole finished playing Bach's English Suite no. 2 in A Minor, the capacity audience that filled Carnegie Recital Hall on Monday evening, October 4, 1971, rose to its feet and gave her a standing ovation.

Miss Cole, who was making her official New York solo debut, began studying the piano in Cleveland, Ohio, at the age of three. She studied both piano and violin at the Cleveland Institute of Music, graduated cum laude from Miami University in Oxford, Ohio, and attended graduate school at Teacher's College of Columbia University in New York City. She is now an assistant professor of music at Queens College.

Her well-chosen program included Bach's Prelude and Fugue in B Minor from the *Well-Tempered Clavichord, Book Two*, five sonatas by Scarlatti, Couperin's *Les Baricades Misterieuses*, Rameau's *Gavotte et Six Doubles* in A Minor,

Bartok's Six Romanian Folk Dances, and Bach's English Suite no. 2 in A Minor.

Although everything was played unusually well, there was one moment during the final movement of the Rameau piece that made it clear to all present that Miss Cole was an extraordinary artist.[4]

Since Miss Cole was the first Black harpsichord player to appear on the American musical scene, a capacity audience filled the hall when she made her New York debut. Her performance far exceeded their expectations, and listeners and critics alike were unanimous in their praise.

The *New York Times* wrote: "She played a difficult program with fluency, flair and imagination. Miss Cole, like most harpsichordists is a passionate soul; unlike most, she reveals it in her performances. . . . All in all, Miss Cole proved herself an artist to keep in mind."

Since that concert, Miss Cole has played over a hundred recitals in England, Germany, and the United States. Yet when she returned to Alice Tully Hall on Sunday, February 23, 1975, the *Times* forgot to keep her in mind. No one covered the recital!

Miss Cole studied both piano and violin. After receiving her graduate degree from Columbia, she went on to get her doctorate. Her advanced harpsichord studies were at the Landowska Center in Connecticut, where she studied with Mme. Denise Restout. She founded the Harpsichord Festival at Westminster Choir College.

V

INSTRUMENTALISTS

48   The African Prince

Around 1789 there appeared on the London scene one John Frederick Bridgetower, who billed himself as an African prince. Traveling with him was his remarkable ten-year-old violin prodigy son, George. Little is known of the young Bridgetower's background except that he was born in Biala, Poland, in 1779, that his mother was a Polish woman, and that his brother was an accomplished cellist. According to the diaries of Mrs. Papendiek, assistant keeper of the wardrobe and reader to the queen, we know that the violinist and his father gave a command performance before King George III at Windsor Royal Lodge. Of this occasion she wrote, "Both father and son pleased greatly. The son for his talent and modest bearing, the father for his fascinating manner, elegance, expertness in all languages, beauty of person and taste in dress. He seemed to win the good opinion of everyone, and was courted by all and entreated to join in society."

Soon after, the Bridgetowers were seen in the fashionable watering place of Bath, where the enterprising father wasted no time in arranging for a public appearance for young

George in the New Assembly Rooms on Saturday, December 5, 1789. The *Bath Journal* reported: "The amateurs of music in this city received on Saturday last at the New Rooms the highest treat imaginable from the exquisite performance of Master Bridgetower, whose taste and execution on the violin is equal, perhaps superior, to the best professor of the present or any former day. The concert room, recesses and gallery were thronged with the very best of company, who were enraptured with the astonishing abilities of this wonderful child."

With the master touch of an impresario, John Bridgetower let just enough time pass for the word to get around fashionable English circles about his young son's success at Bath before he arranged for a London public debut. This occurred on February 19, 1790, when George played a violin solo between parts of the annual performance of Handel's *Messiah* at the Drury Lane Theatre before a distinguished audience. The *London Advertiser* wrote: "Master Bridgetower is a complete master of the violin." The *London Chronicle* reported: "Master Bridgetower performed with great taste and execution." It did not take the Bridgetowers long to become the talk of the town.

Offstage, however, it seems that young George was not happy at all. He confided to Mrs. Papendiek that his mother and brother had been left in distress and that the money earned by his public appearances was being wasted by his father. One evening, after being treated with especial severity by his father, George ran off to Carlton House and asked the Prince of Wales for refuge. The prince immediately sent for John Bridgetower and ordered him to leave the country and took the prodigy into his family circle like a son. The atmosphere of Carlton House was ideal. Here he was not pressed to earn a living through his violin playing and was permitted to develop at his own pace. He came into daily contact with such music masters as Giardini, Cramer, Salomon, and Viotti. By the time he reached the age of fifteen in 1794, he was appointed first violinist in the prince's own private orchestra.

In 1802, the Prince of Wales granted Bridgetower a leave of absence so that he could visit his mother, who was living in Dresden, and to tour the Continent. His appearances there were so successful that he decided to try his luck in Vienna, where his talents came to the attention of Beethoven. Among Beethoven's letters is one dated May 18, 1803, which reads: "Dear Baron von Wetzlar: Although we have never addressed each other, I do not hesitate to recommend to you the bearer, Herr Bridgetower, a very capable virtuoso who has a complete command of his instrument. . . ." Another reads: "My dear Bridgetower, come today at twelve o'clock to Count Deyms where we were together the day before yesterday. They perhaps wish to hear you play something or other, but that you'll find out. I rejoice at the mere thought of seeing you today. Your friend, Beethoven."

In Thayer's famous biography of Beethoven, the story is related that the master originally dedicated his Sonata no. 9 in A Major (Opus 47) to Bridgetower, but a quarrel between the two musicians over a young lady caused Beethoven to change the inscription to Rudolph Kreutzer. Whether this is true or not is less important than the fact that records show that Beethoven and Bridgetower did perform the premiere of this sonata together on May 24, 1803, in the Augartenhalle. There is a curious signed note on the violinist's own copy of the sonata relating to this performance. It reads: "When I accompanied him in this Sonata-Concertante at Wien, at the repetition of the first part of the Presto, I imitated the flight, at the 18th bar, of the pianoforte of this movement. He jumped up, embraced me, saying: 'Noch einmal, mein lieber Bursch!' [Once again, dear boy!] Then he held the open pedal during this flight, the chord of C as at the ninth bar."

In July of 1803, Bridgetower returned to London and to his post in the orchestra of the Prince of Wales. Not content to rest on his laurels, he wisely continued his studies at Cambridge University, from which he was graduated in 1811. One of the compositions which he composed for his final examinations was played at Great St. Mary's Church in Cambridge on June 30, 1811, at the installation of the Duke of Gloucester as chancellor of the university. The *London Times* reported: "The composition was elaborate and rich; and highly accredited to the talents of the graduate. The trio struck us, particularly, by its beauty." He continued to compose after his graduation, and in 1812 he published a manual of study entitled *Diatonica Armonica for the Pianoforte* as well as a ballad, "Henry." This ballad in its original manuscript is now housed in the British Museum.

Very little is known about Bridgetower in later years. He married an Englishwoman whose maiden name was Drake, but it is not known exactly when. Records show that he visited Rome in 1825 and again in 1827. The recent discovery in Italy of the manuscripts of a symphony and a double concerto for violin, cello, and orchestra prove that Bridgetower did a considerable amount of composing. After the death of his patron and guardian George IV, Bridgetower seems to have fallen on hard times. He died on February 29, 1860, at the considerable age of eighty-one.

49   A Master Violinist

"Allow me to express to you all the pleasure that I felt Sunday last at my friend M. David's. The warmth of your execution, the feeling, the elegance, the brilliance of the school to which you belong, show qualities in you as an artist of which the French school may be proud."

This is an excerpt from a note signed by G. Rossini. It is addressed to Jose Silvestre de los Delores White, the Afro-Cuban violinist who dazzled the musical public of Paris in the nineteenth century. He had come to Paris at the suggestion of Louis Moreau Gottschalk.

Born in 1839 in Mantanzas, Cuba, he was the son of a French businessman and amateur violinist and an Afro-Cuban mother. After studying with his father and others, White was sent to Paris to work with Delphin Alard. It is interesting to note that a fellow student at the Conservatoire was Sarasate.

When he competed in a contest at the Conservatoire in 1856, White won the first prize. According to an account in *Le Pays* (August 5, 1856): "He has played with an extraordinary animation, not like a pupil, but like a master—like a great artist who commands his auditory."

Some years later, he appeared as soloist in his own Concerto for Violin and Orchestra. *France Musicale* (March 3, 1867) wrote: "This composition of a high value has been, in one word, the object of a true ovation for M. White, who was both soloist and composer."

At a concert at the Conservatoire in 1872, White played the Mendelssohn Violin Concerto. *Le Siecle* (May 13, 1872) reported: "The virtuoso showed himself the worthy interpreter of the composer . . . his playing was full, correct, warm and well-moderated."

White returned to Cuba in 1875 but was forced to leave by the government after anti-Spanish crowds sang the prohibited "Viva Cuba Libre" at one of his concerts. Shortly after this incident, he came to the United States, where he made several appearances in Boston and New York.

When he played the Mendelssohn concerto with the New York Philharmonic at the Brooklyn Academy of Music, the *New York Times* (December 12, 1875) wrote: "Señor White's delivery was simply perfect, the lovely andante of the composition revealing particularly the sweetness and expressiveness of his cantabile."

The last I have been able to trace of White's career is a record of his having settled in Rio de Janeiro, where he joined Arthur Napoleao in the establishment of the Sociedade de Conciertos Clasicos. He also served as teacher of the children of Emperor Pedro II.

Fortunately, Professor Paul Glass of Brooklyn College found the manuscript of White's Violin Concerto in the Bibliotheque Nationale in Paris and prepared a performance edition. This was played on February 24, 1974, by Ruggiero Ricci and the Symphony of the New World at Avery Fisher Hall.

The *New York Times* (February 25, 1974) wrote: "The most unusual item on the program was unquestionably Joseph White's Violin Concerto in F-sharp Minor. The orchestration is hardly over-complex but is deftly put together and serves as a proper backdrop for the soloist and pyrotechnics. . . ."

50   Kermit Moore at Alice Tully Hall

Kermit Moore, the celebrated Black cellist, returned to Alice Tully Hall at Lincoln Center on Sunday afternoon March 14, 1976 to give a recital equally divided between standard and contemporary works. He was assisted by pianist Patrick Mullins, his frequent collaborator.

Highlighting the program was the first performance of Moore's own Music for Cello and Piano. Divided into three parts, the work remained highly musical in spite of its complexities. Needless to say, the reading of the score was definitive.

Another first performance was Seymour Barab's Allegri for Cello and Piano, written especially for Moore. It turned out to be a series of delightful trifles, skillfully composed. Moore and Mullins brought out the inherent humor in the score and drew much applause from the audience.

As the musical community already knows, Moore is a musician of the highest order and a superb cello player. On this occasion, one could have wished for a little more poetry in the Brahms Sonata in E Minor (Opus 38) and the allegro in the Bach Sonata no. 2 in D Major seemed too fast.

The balance of the program included Edward Margetson's Ballade for Cello and Piano and Chopin's Introduction and Polonaise Brillante (Opus 3). The former proved to be a delight, and one could not ask for a better performance of the Chopin.

In his review in the *New York Post*, Robert Kimball pro-

claimed that "Moore might well have given so much attention to so many worthy enterprises that his skills as cellist
have atrophied a bit."

Well, let *him* try to find a manager for a Black cellist who
prepared himself for a major career and found the doors
closed. And one who, in spite of this fact, has managed to
make a very good living from his musical enterprises. And
one who has elicited rave reviews from critics who are more
distinguished than a second-string pipsqueak from the *Post*.[1]

Under normal circumstances, I would not criticize one of
my colleagues of the press in print. In this case, however, I
felt that it was my moral duty to answer Kimball, if for no
other reason than to set the record straight for my readers
who might have seen his review.

I have watched the career of this remarkable artist from
his student days at the Cleveland Institute of Music, from
where, after he was graduated, he saw many of his colleagues
go on to posts with major orchestras. Because he was Black,
these opportunities were not open to him.

Instead of accepting defeat, he went on to further develop
his musicianship under such masters as Felix Salmond in New
York and Paul Bazelaire, George Enesco, Pierre Pasquier,
and Nadia Boulanger in France. The queen of Belgium was
so impressed with his abilities that she ordered a medal
pressed as tribute.

He is to date the only Black cellist to appear with major
orchestras of the world. He has been soloist with the Orchestre de la Suisse Romande, the Concertgebouw, the National Radio Symphony of Paris, the Belgian National Orchestra, and several orchestras in the United States.

The *Journal de Genève* has said of him, "Kermit Moore is

an accomplished virtuoso. The musician was able to put to use the rich resources of his technique and to give an example of the ease in his elocution, and not less, the moving quality of his sonority."

Besides playing concerts, he was active in founding the Symphony of the New World and the Society of Black Composers. He has conducted some orchestral concerts and has tried his hand at composing. His Music for Cello and Piano, performed at Alice Tully Hall, March 14, 1976, received high critical acclaim.

When the day comes that Black instrumentalists are accepted on the American concert stage, Kermit Moore will be remembered as a hero, a pioneer. The names of his detractors will be at that time only bylines that have absolutely no meaning to those who might encounter them.

51   Distinguished Music-Making

Alice Tully Hall is too new to be permeated with those mystical *echoes du temps passé* that distinguish the great concert rooms of the world. Yet, at the Sunday afternoon, May 23, 1976 Triad presentation, violinist Sanford Allen and soprano Miriam Burton evoked spirits of the past.

It was altogether fitting that Allen should open the concert with a sonata by Jean-Marie Leclair (1697–1764). He was one of the teachers of the Black violinist-composer Chevalier de Saint-Georges (1739–1799), who captured the imagination of all of France in the eighteenth century.

Throughout the concert, Allen's playing was cool and elegant with a burning musical spirit simmering underneath. This proved perfectly suited to Brahms' Sonata no. 2 in A Major (Opus 100). Pianist Warren Wilson matched Allen's superb musicianship phrase by phrase.

Another high point was Allen and Wilson's playing of a sonatina by the Black Panamanian composer Roque Cordero, filled with exciting Latin rhythms and dissonances. Allen's complete identification with this music stems from his highly praised recording of Cordero's Concerto for Violin on Columbia Records.

One has to look back to the famous Debussy song recording by Maggie Teyte and Alfred Cortot as a frame of reference to appreciate the marvelous sense of style exhibited by soprano Miriam Burton and pianist Kelley Wyatt in Debussy's seven *Ariettes Oubliées*, based on poetry by Paul Verlaine.

Composed in the year 1888, they were originally titled simply *Ariettes*, later changed for publication and dedicated to the legendary Mary Garden. Miss Burton brought a vocal opulence to the music that topped her predecessors, with just a shade of edginess marring the top notes.

Wilson, Burton, and Allen combined their forces to perform the premiere of Dorothy Rudd Moore's moving *Sonnets on Love, Rosebuds and Death*. The carefully chosen texts were culled from works by Alice Dunbar Nelson, Clarissa Scott Delaney, Gwendolyn B. Bennet, Langston Hughes, and Arna Bontemps.

Although Miss Moore expresses herself within the framework of conventional musical means, she has an individual style. Her cycle was given an inspired performance and, judg-

ing from audience response, it will find its way to many concert programs in the future.[2]

Fifteen years ago, violinist Sanford Allen became the first
Black member of the New York Philharmonic. Since that
time, he has played several major recitals in the metropolitan
area as well as making a highly acclaimed debut as soloist
in the Roque Cordero Violin Concerto on Columbia Records.
This latter success has resulted in his being invited to be
soloist with such major orchestras as the Detroit Symphony
and L'Orchestre Symphonique de Quebec. He has just resigned from his post with the Philharmonic and is about to
embark on a career as the first major Black concert violinist.
The following is an interview I had with him in his New
York apartment.

Abdul: What should happen to your career now that you
are free to devote your entire time to solo playing?

Allen: Because my situation seems to be unusual in a number of ways, it is really hard to say. In spite of my success as
a solo player, it seems to be very difficult for me to gain any
momentum.

Abdul: Do you think that your coming appearance as a
soloist with the Philharmonic will make a difference?

Allen: Hopefully it will make a dent in somebody's con-
sciousness.

Abdul: Isn't it almost impossible for a violinist to make a
living exclusively by playing concerts?

Allen: I think that it depends on who is giving the concerts. There are a few rare birds who manage it.

Abdul: Would you settle for a career which involves playing some engagements and being an artist-in-residence somewhere?

Allen: I have always been fairly flexible in how I earn a living. I've spent a lot of time in the recording studios here in New York. I am not opposed to the idea in general, but it would have to be under the right circumstances.

Abdul: When you first began preparing for your career, did you ever stop and think whether or not there would be job opportunities for a Black?

Allen: Fortunately, I did not think about that. I was simply preoccupied with music as being something that I wanted to do. I simply wanted to play the violin.

Abdul: How did the Philharmonic job present itself?

Allen: I was told that the job could be available. It involved a lot of discussions because, at that time, it was a fairly thorny issue. In a sense, I wound up being the guinea pig. The first time I auditioned, I did not get into the orchestra, but wound up playing a summer season at Lewisohn Stadium. Then I auditioned again, which resulted in my playing as a substitute for a player who was ill. The following season, I actually joined the orchestra as a regular member.

Abdul: I understand that you have a very special instrument. Could you tell me something about it?

Allen: Well, it is a Stradivarius, dated 1714, and it is a lovely instrument. It has a strong sound and it's very responsive. It allows one to operate on a wider range of colors than is possible with some other instruments. I also find it very dependable. I find that if anything goes wrong it is usually my fault and not the instrument.

Abdul: What does the effect of being an artist and also a spokesman for a group of people have on your music-making?

Allen: I try and divorce the two. At this point in my life, I feel that I have to deal with things in the order of priorities. My major obligation is to myself in the sense that I have functioned as a symbol for a long time now. At this point, I want to devote my time to solo playing so I have to concentrate my energy in this direction.

Abdul: You are really at a very exciting point in your career now, and the possibilities seem to be infinite.

Allen: They are either infinite or nonexistent—I can't tell which. I find the whole thing totally unpredictable. There is a certain amount of drama involved, and I really don't know what is on the next page.

VI

CONDUCTORS, ORCHESTRAS, AND CHORUSES

52 Dean Dixon: A First

When Dean Dixon returned to the United States after a twenty-one-year absence to conduct the New York Philharmonic in Central Park in the summer of 1970, an audience of seventy-five thousand people gathered to welcome him home. Of this occasion, *Newsweek* reported: "He is no showboat conductor, yet he showered his program (Henze, Sibelius, and Brahms) with a lilting lyricism and controlled grace. And he gave Brahms' Second Symphony a rich romantic sweep that brought the great throng to its feet in a standing, especially thrilling ovation." This was the long overdue reward for a brave, fifty-five-year-old man who dared to become the first full-time black American conductor of symphonic music.

Born in Harlem on January 10, 1915, Dixon is the son of Henry Charles and McClara (Rolston) Dixon, both of whom came from the West Indies. From an early age, his mother took him to concerts in Carnegie Hall, where he was exposed to the finest music and musicians. While he was a student at DeWitt Clinton High School, he organized his own amateur orchestra, which proved so successful that the head of the music department urged him to devote himself to a musical career. Upon graduation, he enrolled at Juilliard, from which he received his B.S. degree. He entered the graduate school and also attended Columbia University Teachers College, from which he received his M.A.

After years of conducting various orchestras that he personally organized, he was chosen by Samuel Chotzinoff to direct the NBC Summer Symphony for two concerts in 1941. The *New York Times* wrote: "The men gave him everything he asked for. He knew exactly what he wanted and wasted no time talking. From the very beginning he was master of the situation." Return engagements followed, and he soon added the New York Philharmonic (Lewisohn Stadium), the Philadelphia Orchestra (Robin Hood Dell), and the Boston Symphony to his credits. But by the time he received the Alice Ditson Award for Outstanding Contributions to American Music in 1948, the opportunities had dwindled down to none. "It suddenly dawned on me that those first opportunities were a gesture in the coming confrontations between Black and white America," he told a magazine. "I suppose I could have enlisted the help of the teeth people—the NAACP and Urban League—but I wanted my music, not my color, to open doors." He decided to leave for Europe.

Instead of wallowing in bitterness, he proceeded to build a solid career for himself abroad, and by 1952 he had reached the point where he presented in one season alone forty-four American works by twenty-five composers with major orchestras. In a glowing article in the *New York Herald Tribune* of March 23, 1952, Virgil Thomson wrote: "Dean Dixon, among all the American conductors who since the war have traveled professionally in foreign lands, has been our most assiduous ambassador of American music. . . . Press and public in Europe, as here, have consistently demonstrated their confidence in Mr. Dixon's high skill and in his unusual warmth of temperament, his classical culture. But he has used his distinguished abilities not only to prove abroad that Americans can conduct but also to prove that they can write music."

By 1953, Dixon was invited to become artistic and musical director of the Göteborg Symphony Orchestra in Sweden, a post which he held until 1960. During the period from 1961–1971, he served as musical director of the Hessischer Rundfunk Orchestra in Frankfurt-am-Main, Germany. Because of the differences in seasons between Germany and Australia, it was possible for him also to serve as musical director of the Sydney Symphony Orchestra from 1964–1967 without interrupting his work in Frankfurt. But in a recent article, he admitted that his happiest periods have been with a single orchestra. He told the reporter, "By nature I'm a builder."

The general sentiments of observers of the black musical scene were beautifully summed up in a review of Dixon's return to the Philadelphia Orchestra. In the *Evening Bulletin* of April 4, 1975, James Felton wrote: "Last night, he was greeted by audience and the Philadelphia Orchestra players alike with an affectionate, respectful ovation reserved for the real musical heroes of this world. . . . Dean Dixon is still very much a conductor to reckon with. A permanent major post should be open to him in his own country. His belated debut with the Philadelphia Orchestra was brilliant and exciting."

Dixon died in November of 1976 in Zurich, Switzerland, at the age of sixty-one. He is survived by his wife, Titha, and two daughters. The Symphony of the New World under Everett Lee played the Brahms Fourth Symphony in his memory at its November concert that year.

53   Everett Lee's Philharmonic Debut

When Everett Lee stepped onstage to make his conducting debut with the New York Philharmonic at Avery Fisher Hall on Thursday evening, January 15, 1976, my gut reaction was that he was responding to a long overdue invitation tendered by a somewhat reluctant host who was trying to ease his own conscience.

After all, it was only twenty-eight years ago that Lee made an auspicious New York debut as leader of the Cosmopolitan Little Symphony at Town Hall. And in the interim he only served as musical director of the Norrköping Symphony (Sweden) for ten years, made guest appearances all over the world, and became musical director of the Symphony of the New World.

If Lee had any feelings of animosity that Thursday, it certainly didn't show when he opened the program with *Kosbro* (Keep on steppin', brothers) by the young Black composer David Baker. It is a joyful, brilliantly orchestrated work deeply rooted in the Afro-American and African musical tradition. As its title suggests, forget bygones and move on to the *now*.

With Ruggiero Ricci as soloist, the program continued with Sibelius' Concerto for Violin and Orchestra in D Minor (Opus 47). Despite some pitch problems, Ricci played with a big, warm tone, great technical virtuosity, and marvelous vitality. Lee, also a trained violinist, led the orchestra in the kind of accompaniment that allowed the soloist room to assert his own personality.

The program closed with Rachmaninoff's Symphony no. 3

in A Minor (Opus 44), a work which usually suffers from too somber a reading. Wisely, Lee chose to bring out the cheerful aspects of the score. It unfolded at an unhurried pace and one had a feeling of well-being throughout the performance.

At the close of the concert, the Philharmonic audience gave Lee a rather cool reception. This may be partially due to the fact that he did not try to dazzle them with artificial theatrics. Another reason may be that he was not "packaged" by Madison Avenue. In any case, he certainly makes beautiful music.[1]

Everett Lee's career as a conductor has taken him to major orchestras and opera houses throughout the world. A graduate of the Cleveland Institute of Music, he also studied with such masters as Mitropoulos, Rudolf, and Walter. He served as chief conductor of the Norrköping Symphony in Sweden for a decade, as well as holding a post with the Royal Swedish Opera. His numerous appearances in the United States include the San Francisco Opera, Cincinnati Opera, Cleveland Symphony, Dallas Symphony, St. Louis Symphony, Baltimore Symphony, and the New York Philharmonic. He is presently musical director of the Symphony of the New World. Here is an excerpt from a recent conversation I had with him in New York.

Abdul: I understand that you began your career as a violinist, not a conductor. When you were a student at the Cleveland Institute, did you ever think about the fact that there were no opportunities for a Black concert violinist?

Lee: It was uppermost in my mind, but, like most young people, I thought that I could go out and conquer the world.

Abdul: What actually happened after you were graduated from music school?

Lee: Not too much, to be frank with you. Naturally, I wanted to play with the Cleveland Orchestra like all the other fellows who had come out of my class.

Abdul: Who was the conductor at that time?

Lee: Artur Rodzinski. I remember being in touch with him later in New York when I wanted to audition for the Philharmonic. He was afraid to encourage me to try because he didn't want me to be hurt. He knew that I would not be accepted into the orchestra. This was one of the factors which helped me decide to try conducting. Then Leonard Bernstein and Boris Goldovsky encouraged me to take the conducting classes at Tanglewood. I also went to the Juilliard Summer School and Columbia for further work.

Abdul: Actually, it is not unusual for a violinist to become a conductor. In the eighteenth century, the first violinist was what we now know as a conductor.

Lee: That's true. But, in any case, some of the musicians with whom I worked encouraged me to continue conducting, especially opera. When I was in Europe on a West German grant, I conducted for a traveling opera company. This gave me the opportunity to cover a large part of the standard repertory. In between operas, I made guest appearances with orchestras in Brussels, Berlin, and elsewhere. After some guest work in Scandinavia, I was offered the post of chief conductor at Norrköping where I stayed for ten years.

Abdul: When did you return to the United States?

Lee: Around 1970, I began to get offers from Sixten Ehrling in Detroit, Max Rudolf in Cincinnati, Robert Shaw in Atlanta, and Baltimore.

Abdul: When did you come to the Symphony of the New World?

Lee: At first I came several times as guest conductor. I

was invited by an old friend of mine, Benjamin Steinberg, one of the orchestra's founders. Then, in 1973, I was invited to become musical director.

Abdul: What are your plans for the Symphony of the New World?

Lee: One of the things we must do is to let the public know about the orchestra. We need exposure in the news media. And we need financial backing. This orchestra has enormous possibilities. One of the goals is to be able to have a season with enough concerts to make it possible to maintain the same personnel for each concert. This will give the orchestra a unity.

Abdul: What responsibility do you think the orchestra has to Black composers?

Lee: This is nothing new to me. I have done many Black composers throughout my career. I have conducted works by Mark Fax, Ulysses Kay, and David Baker. Next season I plan to devote three of our six programs exclusively to American composers.

Abdul: Along with Dean Dixon, you have been a pioneer in the field of conducting for Blacks. How do you feel about the fact that there are now many young Blacks getting the opportunity to conduct major orchestras?

Lee: I think that it's wonderful. It was really a thrill recently for me to hear James De Preist conducting a Mahler symphony. He has never had the Central European experience, yet here was an American conducting a work which is so very Austrian in spirit, and his interpretation was truly remarkable.

54 Henry Lewis: Another First

"Henry Lewis today became the first Negro appointed music director of a symphony orchestra in the United States. The 36-year-old Mr. Lewis will head the New Jersey Symphony effective June 1." Thus began an article in the *New York Times* dated February 16, 1968.

When the president of the orchestra's board was asked whether Lewis's race had any bearing on his appointment, he answered, "Almost none until we came down to the final selection and realized that Mr. Lewis was the best qualified of all the candidates."

Lewis first came into national prominence when he substituted for an ailing Igor Markevitch in a pair of Los Angeles Philharmonic concerts in 1961. This led to his being appointed assistant conductor of the orchestra for a year at the beginning of Zubin Mehta's tenure as musical director. Prior to that, Lewis had played for a number of years as a double bass player with the orchestra.

In 1959, he founded the Los Angeles Chamber Orchestra, which in 1963 toured Europe under the auspices of the State Department. He also conducted an orchestra during military service.

When Lewis took over the New Jersey Symphony, it was a pickup group of semiprofessional musicians, playing twenty-two concerts a season. Three years later, under his direction, it was enlarged to eighty-seven professionals playing more than a hundred concerts a season.

In fact, in a feature article in the *New York Times* dated March 5, 1971, Lewis was able to exclaim proudly: "To have formed an orchestra like this one—in America today, when symphony orchestras everywhere else are in trouble and cutting back—is a miracle."

In October of 1968, Lewis chalked up another first—he became the first Black to conduct at the Metropolitan Opera. The opera was *La Boheme,* and one major critic wrote that "the Puccini style of broad lyricism was one he understood well and could command technically."

Lewis is no longer with the New Jersey Symphony. He now devotes his time to conducting at the Metropolitan Opera, where he recently scored a personal success leading a new production of *Le Prophete* in which his wife, Marilyn Horne, sang the role of Fides. He also finds time to accept engagements as guest conductor with leading orchestras around the world.

55   James De Preist: A Portrait

Philadelphia-born James De Preist is musical director of L'Orchestre Symphonique de Quebec, one of the handful of Blacks to hold such a position. He has also been assistant conductor of the New York Philharmonic and associate conductor of the National Symphony. A first-prize winner of the Mitropoulos International Conductors Competition, he has appeared as guest conductor with such important European orchestras as those at Rotterdam, Stockholm, Brussels, and

Berlin. In the United States he has been guest conductor of major orchestras, including those of New York, Philadelphia, Chicago, Pittsburgh, Minnesota, Cleveland, Boston, Los Angeles, as well as the Symphony of the New World (New York). The following excerpts from a conversation in his New York apartment take the reader into the fascinating world of an outstanding young American conductor.

Abdul: Did the fact that your aunt, Marian Anderson, was one of the world's most famous singers have any bearing on your choice of making a career in music?

De Preist: Well, I lived in a very musical home. I studied piano like most young people did at that time. My mother was also a fine singer, and there were always recordings in the home. There was a tradition of listening to opera and to concert broadcasts, but I don't recall any special impact that music made upon me.

Abdul: So nobody tried to force music on you?

De Preist: No. The result of that nonforcing was that I went into the University of Pennsylvania and worked toward a degree in economics because I planned to be a lawyer. I hadn't the slightest idea of pursuing music as a career. I remember that when I was in high school, however, Dr. Lewis Werson got many of us who eventually went into music "hooked" because of his enthusiasm. I played tympani and percussion in the All-Philadelphia Senior High School Orchestra. If there was any planting of a seed, performing-wise, it was in the course of being in the orchestra in Philadelphia schools.

Abdul: Did you continue your musical pursuits at college?

De Preist: While I was at Penn, I was taking electives in the music department. And I was also actively involved with jazz, presenting a series of concerts utilizing jazz and non-jazz elements and lighting—it was a mixed media thing—but still this was an avocation. After I was graduated from Penn, I was commissioned to write a ballet score for the Philadelphia Dance Company, which I accepted. By 1959, I decided that I would go to the Philadelphia Conservatory and take some select courses in harmony and orchestration and study composition with Vincent Persichetti. Still, I was so undecided about entering music that I went on to graduate school and got a master's degree in communications. Then, the State Department asked me if I would be interested in doing a tour as an American specialist in the Far and Near East in 1962.

Abdul: Did you accept that offer?

De Preist: I accepted the tour, and the first stop was Bangkok. Ostensibly the purpose there was to work with the jazz musicians, due to the influence of the king, who was an amateur saxophonist and clarinet player. By accident, I found that there was a symphony orchestra connected with the Ministry of Culture. I asked a friend of mine to take me to a rehearsal. They were preparing the Schubert C Major Symphony, and they asked me if I would rehearse with them. I had never, of course, conducted that symphony, but it was one of several albums my aunt had given me as a teen-ager and to which I had listened. The musicians responded to what I was doing. Everything felt so natural about the music. I discovered at that point that *that* was what I wanted to do.

Abdul: When you made this decision, did you ever stop to think that the possibilities were very limited for a Black conductor?

De Preist: From junior high school forward, I never thought anything about being inhibited from doing anything I wanted to do. A major problem at that time was to find out how significant the ability was. In ascertaining this, I continued on the tour to places where the orchestras were better, and the same thing happened—the musicians responded.

Abdul: Wasn't it in Thailand that you came down with polio?

De Preist: One morning when I got up, I couldn't put any pressure on the bottom of my right foot and I came down with a fever. I went to the doctor, and he gave me something to bring down the fever and told me to go to bed. The next morning I couldn't stand up, so I called the embassy and they sent over a doctor and I went to the hospital for tests. He came back to me and said, "I have bad news for you. You have polio."

[De Preist was flown back to Philadelphia where he began his long road to recovery. Besides learning to walk again, he plunged himself into preparations for the 1963 Mitropoulos International Conductors Competition, which he was determined to enter.]

I was rather apprehensive about what was going to happen when I went to New York for the competition because I thought that they would have all the hotshot young American conductors who had been in Europe. So I went in and I conducted the first movement of the Tchaikowsky *Pathetique*. This was my first opportunity before a professional American orchestra doing music of the standard repertory. Needless to say, I had never conducted any of these things before. It was exactly the same as it had been before every place else in the course of the tour, except that the sound was glorious and I *knew* that I could do it. So, of the hundred American conductors to whom they listened, there were seven who were picked to represent the United States, and I was one of the seven. By the time we reached the semifinals, there were only two Americans left and neither of us went byond that.

[In 1964, DePreist entered the competition again and emerged as a first-prize winner. After a season as an assistant conductor of the New York Philharmonic (1965–1966) he found himself with no prospects for the future. He and his wife moved to Rotterdam, Holland, where his friend Edo De Waart was conductor of the orchestra.]

In December of 1967, my friend Edo De Waart called me and told me that he had to be in London during the 1968–1969 season and he could not do four of his concerts in Rotterdam scheduled for February. He asked the management to let me do them. That was to be my European debut. It is very rare at that point in careers that conductors help each other.

Abdul: I know. It is a question of self-preservation.

De Preist: Literally everything was hinging on the success of that debut concert in Rotterdam. It couldn't be a modest success or just good results, but everything had to be absolutely sensational.

Abdul: You must have felt like a circus performer.

De Preist: In a way I did. I thought to myself: "This is really insane. I have to eat and survive and it's dependent upon how well a lot of people I've never met respond to me on the platform and how people write about me in the newspaper.

Abdul: Was the concert a success?

De Preist: It was everything I could hope for—plus some. *Everything* followed. The next concerts I did were in Stockholm. Rotterdam re-engaged me for five or six concerts. In Stockholm, *that* success was even greater than Rotterdam. Two weeks later Rafael Kubelik got ill, and I went back to Stockholm to replace him and work with Andre Watts for the first time. And that cemented my success in Stockholm and resulted in my returning every year for longer periods. I went on to Belgium, Germany, and Italy. Then a letter came from the Hurok office—"Dear Jimmy . . ." [Sol Hurok, who had managed his famous aunt's career, was prepared to take over his.]

[On both sides of the Atlantic, more and more engagements followed. One of the most memorable, however, was the opportunity to conduct the National Symphony in Washington, D.C., in Constitution Hall, where, many years before, his aunt was refused the right to sing.]

De Preist: Antal Dorati asked me to come to Washington to conduct the National Symphony in 1970, when they were still in Constitution Hall. That was a very emotional moment because that was the same hall where my aunt could *not* appear. But it was so *simple* for me. I just went in and walked out on the stage. That was a very special moment.

Abdul: Was she present on that occasion?

De Preist: No, but I called her the night after the first rehearsal and told her how I felt.

[Not long after that appearance, De Preist was engaged by the National Symphony as its associate conductor.]

Abdul: When you are confronted with the question of the relevance of European symphonic music to Blacks, how do you handle it?

De Preist: Music, whether or not it happens to be Western European, is for human beings. It can be enlightening, enriching. It can be a meaningful encounter regardless of racial, ethnic, or national orientation. But for Blacks in America, there is nothing that is alien in classical music in terms of its essence. What one wants to get in the soul of Beethoven is as easily perceived and is as relevant to a Black human being as to a white human being, because the *soul* of Beethoven, the *soul* of Mozart, the *soul* of Brahms, or *any* composer of *any* music speaks directly to the human heart. It penetrates through all the layers of superficiality, all of the layers of accumulated doctrine, all of the layers of acculturation—it gets to you in essence where you are just like everyone else. The first experience is the human experience, which transcends race, so that pain, happiness, depression, exultation—all of the basic human emotions that have nothing to do with race—are affected by music. The Black experience is on top of this, which gives a special character. If I find something that is elevating or that elates me, the way which I will vocally manifest that will be entirely different from a white person's expression. The way I will show *my* grief or anger will be different, but the anger and the grief and the exultation are fundamental human emotions, and these are the emotions that I try to touch—have the music touch—and convey *that* to audiences. And, in that sense, classical music is relevant to anyone who wants to give himself over to it.

56   Symphony of the New World

When the Symphony of the New World began its eleventh season on Sunday afternoon, November 7, 1976, in Carnegie Hall, it offered music by Mendelssohn, Saint-Saens, and Brahms under the direction of the Black conductor Everett Lee with pianist Lorin Hollander as guest soloist.

On the surface, one might get the impression that this was just another fine musical event being offered by just another fine orchestra. Nothing could be further from the truth. One of the differences was the presence of Black musicians who made up almost half of the personnel.

A recent survey showed that among fifty-four American symphonic orchestras which hire 4,690 musicians on a regular basis, only 67 were from minority groups. In some cases, it has taken the threat of a lawsuit to get the management to even consider auditioning a Black instrumentalist.

Another thing that distinguishes the Symphony of the New World from other institutions is that its musical director is Black. At present, conductor Everett Lee is the only Black holding such a position with a major American orchestra. In Canada, James De Preist has a similar post.

Besides providing employment to Black and other minority musicians, the Symphony of the New World has also provided a forum for Black composers to hear their works performed. Such major composers as William Grant Still, Howard Swanson, and Ulysses Kay have been featured.

Up to that time, the big foundations had given money to the orchestra, but they were all beginning to ask for hard figures on the amount of community support. The life of the Symphony of the New World depended on filling those seats in Carnegie Hall that Sunday.[2]

The Symphony of the New World was founded in 1964 by an interracial committee of musicians. It included Alfred Brown, Selwart R. Clarke, Arthur Davis, Richard Davis, Lucille Dixon, Elayne Jones, Harold M. Jones, Frederick L. King, Kermit Moore, Coleridge-Taylor Perkinson, Ross C. Shub, Harry M. Smyles, Benjamin Steinberg, and Joseph B. Wilder. Throughout this volume there are numerous references to its activities which give the reader a good idea of the extent of its accomplishments.

It should be understood that there have been other important attempts to establish Black symphony orchestras over the years. In 1905, the Philadelphia Concert Orchestra was founded with E. Gilbert Anderson as its conductor. It gave concerts for a number of years with such outstanding Black soloists as violinist Clarence Cameron White and cellist Marion Cumbo.

In 1948, a group of mostly Black music lovers founded the Cosmopolitan Little Symphony Orchestra in New York City. Its conductor was Everett Lee. Besides giving concerts within the Black community, it made an auspicious debut at Town Hall, highly praised by the press.

57 Hall Johnson Remembered

My favorite story about Hall Johnson (1888–1970) centers on a rehearsal of his famous choir. He wanted it to sing pianissimo, but it continued to sing with full-throated vigor. He proceeded to chide it gently: "Children, you don't have to shout to make the Lord hear you!"

Although he organized the first Hall Johnson Choir in 1925, it was not until it appeared in *The Green Pastures* on Broadway in 1930 that it gained national celebrity. It garnered further garlands in Johnson's own play *Run Little Chillun* (1933), and in movie and concert appearances.

In his *Notes on the Negro Spiritual* (1965) Johnson recalls: "We wanted to show how the American Negro slaves created, propagated, and illuminated an art-form which was, and still is, unique in the world of music." He felt strongly that this tradition could only be learned by imitation.

The so-called *Green Pastures* spirituals were recorded in 1938 by RCA Victor, but they have long disappeared from the catalogue. This is most unfortunate, because these were the only authentic professionally sung performances of Afro-American spirituals in their original form.

Fortunately, Hall Johnson edited a volume of *The Green Pastures Spirituals* and it is still available. He also arranged and edited a volume of spirituals for solo voice and piano. These may be the finest arrangements ever made for standard concert use.

Before he died, Hall Johnson was the recipient of many honors. In 1962 Mayor Robert F. Wagner presented him with a citation from the City of New York for his contributions to the cultural life of our city. And again, in 1970, Mayor John V. Lindsay awarded him the Handel Medal.

58   Eva Jessye Is Honored

Eva Jessye was honored at a luncheon at the New York Hilton on Sunday October 10, 1976 by a group of distinguished musicians and friends. She was the first Black woman to gain international acclaim as a choral director, and it would take more space than I have at my disposal to list her achievements.

She is best known to New Yorkers for her magnificent choruses in the premieres of Virgil Thomson's opera *Four Saints*

in Three Acts and George Gershwin's opera *Porgy and Bess.*
For many years, a revival of these works without Miss Jessye
was unthinkable.

A native of Coffeyville, Kansas, she attended Western University (Quindaro, Kansas) and Langston University (Langston, Kansas), holding degrees from both. She was later
awarded a Doctor of Determination degree from the University of Michigan.

Her first important post was that of music director at Morgan State College in Baltimore, where she organized its first
choir. She also coached another local choral group for a New
York audition, which resulted in an appearance at the Rivoli
Theatre.

But her greatest achievement was the Eva Jessye Choir,
which toured from coast to coast for many seasons. Besides
its appearances in the Thomson and Gershwin operas, it was
also featured on radio, in motion pictures, and with the New
York Philharmonic and Minneapolis orchestras.

In recent years, Miss Jessye has shared her knowledge of
Black choral tradition with young people at many colleges
and universities. And she has donated her entire body of
memorabilia to the University of Michigan, where the Eva
Jessye Collection of Afro-American Music has been established.

At the luncheon honoring Miss Jessye, there were the usual
tributes, plaques, and other citations. But, I thought the most
touching moment was when the many musicians who had
worked with her at one time or another gathered on stage to
sing "I'm on My Way" from *Porgy and Bess.*[3]

The Eva Jessye Choir can be heard on the so-called original
cast recording of *Porgy and Bess,* which has been re-released

on MCA Records (MCA-2035). For some unknown reason, Todd Duncan sings both Porgy and Sportin' Life and Anne Brown sings Bess, Clara, and Serena. However, this does not diminish the effect of the fine choral work.

59   An Award for Leonard de Paur

When Leonard de Paur received the annual Harold Jackman Memorial Committee Award on April 12, 1964, we were reminded again of his outstanding contribution to the Black choral tradition. He took the tools he acquired as assistant to Hall Johnson and added a new dimension.

A native of Summit, New Jersey, he is of French Guianian ancestry. He attended Columbia University and the Institute of Musical Art (now Juilliard), after which he became Hall Johnson's assistant. He also served as a director of a unit of the Federal Theatre project.

During a stint in the infantry in the forties, De Paur was assigned to leadership of an all-male chorus, and it was this group which eventually became his famous De Paur Infantry Chorus. It became Columbia Artists' busiest attraction and in 1950 it broke all records with 180 engagements.

When it made its New York debut at Carnegie Hall on January 8, 1950, Olin Downes (*The New York Times*) wrote: "It is one of the best trained choral ensembles now before the public. In point of balance, tone quality, rhythmic precision and shading, its singing is exemplary."

During the 1957–1958 season, he produced the De Paur Opera Gala, which was made up of capsule versions of operas associated with Blacks. This was followed by the De Paur Gala, which included choral masterpieces on the program. After a two-year period of research, he reorganized the De Paur Chorus in 1963.

Unlike his predecessors, de Paur does not lean heavily on Afro-American folk songs in his programming. He puts together exciting programs that cover everything from Palestrina to contemporary American music.[4]

The De Paur Chorus continued to tour through 1969. It was chosen in 1966 to participate in the First World Festival of Negro Arts in Dakar, Senegal, where it was received with great success. This was followed by a fifteen-country tour of Africa, after which they returned to the United States.

De Paur is now director of Community Relations at Lincoln Center, where he has also produced several unusual events. He has also found time to continue conducting. He has been guest conductor of a number of orchestras as well as Opera-South in Jackson, Mississippi.

60   Triad and the Black Vocal Quality

Black singing voices possess a special timbre unmatched by any other ethnic group. When combined into a group effort such as the Triad Chorale, which gave a concert under the auspices of Triad Presentations, Inc., on Sunday afternoon, June 6, 1976, at Alice Tully Hall, the results can be extraordinary.

For many years, Black musicians used to be quite annoyed

when white critics referred to their voices as being "negroid." Many rushed to the nearest conservatory and paid hundreds of hard-earned dollars to train that quality out pronto. It was considered by many to be a fault.

A handful of Black scholars such as Dr. Frederick Hall of Dillard University made serious studies of this "negroid" quality and insisted that their students utilize it in their approach to all music. They knew that it was a treasure and made it their life's work to preserve it.

Conductor Noel da Costa took all of this into consideration and simply played his chorale like a rare musical instrument. And it was its remarkable choral singing that saved a program mostly made up of well-crafted but rather ordinary musical compositions.

William Grant Still, in whose honor the concert was offered, was best represented by his fine solo cycle *Songs of Separation*. They were beautifully performed by soprano Diane Randolph and tenor John Morrison with the assistance of pianist Marjorie De Lewis.

Musically, the high point in the choral part of the program was a group of works by Ulysses Kay, Arthur Cunningham, James Bland, T. Rasul Hakim, and William Lawrence. With percussion played by Wilson Moorman, Hakim's *Tone Prayers*, in its New York premiere, turned out to be a striking and lively work.

It would be criminal not to mention the way Miss De Lewis handled the magnificent piano part in Howard Swanson's art song "Joy" to a Langston Hughes text. For this, she received a well-deserved ovation from the audience. Songs by Still, Margaret Bonds, and William Lawrence completed that group.

The New York premiere of Still's choral suite *From a Lost*

Continent (1948) featured the Chuck Davis Dance Company. It was a valiant effort to breathe life into a dull piece. It was the fine musicianship of the chorale and the special "negroid" vocal quality that gave this program its distinction, not the music.[5]

VII

DIVERTISSEMENTS

61 Harlem Gets a Concert Series

When I first came to New York, I was both surprised and disappointed to find that the Harlem community, which had produced so many fine musicians, offered few opportunities for these artists to appear after they gained prominence. They were all performing downtown.

One afternoon, I sat in the studio of Dr. Clarence Cameron White and I listened with wide-eyed wonder as he spoke of Harlem's glorious past. He spoke of the fine Educational Concert Series presented by Minnie Brown and Daisy Tapley and the Negro String Quartet with Hall Johnson, Marion Cumbo, Felix Weir, and Arthur Boyd. Where were these projects now?

It was this void that stimulated me to create Coffee Concerts, the four-event series which began in November 1958 in the Little Theatre of St. Martin's Episcopal Church. The programs included: November 7—cellist Marion Cumbo, soprano Charlotte Holloman, and pianist Margaret Bonds; December 12—pianist Natale Hinderas; January 16—bass-baritone Edward Lee Tyler and pianist Heinz Hammerman; and February 20—mezzo soprano Betty Allen.

Since I had come out of "the Karamu experience" (Karamu House is an interracial center in Cleveland), I wanted these concerts to be a place where musicians and audiences of all races could come together to share the musical experience. The name Coffee Concerts was chosen because, following the programs, audience and musicians would meet for a cup of coffee.

I asked a number of community leaders to help me bring the series to the attention of the public. This committee was made up of Mrs. Count Basie, Margaret Bonds, Alfred Duckett, Nora Holt, Langston Hughes, Hall Johnson, and Dr. Clarence Cameron White. I assumed the post of director.

The programs which we offered were not a mere carbon copy of downtown concerts, but especially designed to meet the needs of our community. They featured the finest musicians available and subscriptions were available at a price everyone could afford.[1]

Coffee Concerts continued to draw capacity audiences for a total of three seasons. Its final season was devoted to works by Black composers as well as compositions by white composers that reflected the Black spirit. After its final program in 1963, its loss was mourned by an editorial in the *Amsterdam News*. As far as I know, it was the only attempt to establish a professional subscription series in the Harlem community.

62   The Cumbos: Living Music History

Tucked away in a charming little apartment overlooking Central Park are a remarkable couple, Marion and Clarissa Cumbo, who celebrated their fiftieth anniversary in

1976. Both of them have played an important part in the musical life of the Black community since the 1900s.

A concert cellist, Marion has appeared as a soloist as well as a member of several orchestras. Clarissa, who was trained as a singer, has devoted most of her attention to organizational activities. She has been involved in almost every major musical project in the community.

As you enter their apartment, there is a long narrow hallway lined with framed photographs of some of the fine musicians whose lives they have touched. These include Pablo Casals, William Grant Still, Hall Johnson, Kermit Moore, Ronald Lipscomb, and the Negro String Quartet.

At the end of the hall is a small dining room that has been turned into an office where Clarissa can keep an eye on her cooking while she works minor miracles as an impresario. The living room is dominated by a piano, shelves of rare books on Black culture, and Marion's beloved cello.

This lucky visitor was ushered into the parlor where the Cumbos took time off from their busy schedule to share their half century of musical experiences. Soon the personalities behind the numerous photographs began to come vividly to life in tales told with warmth, humor and affection.

I mentioned William Grant Still, the composer who was given a birthday tribute recently at Alice Tully Hall by Clarissa's Triad Presentations. She recalled: "We met him in the twenties, when he was a struggling composer and oboe player. He played in the pit orchestra of such shows as *Shuffle Along*."

Of the Negro String Quartet, which once accompanied Roland Hayes in 1925 at Carnegie Hall, Marion had fond memories. "We wanted to show people that Negroes could do something else besides commit the crimes so often attributed to us in the newspapers in those times," he said.

Besides Marion, the quartet consisted of Felix Weir as first violinist, Arthur Boyd as second violinist, and Hall Johnson as violist. He related: "I had the great honor and privilege to play with those wonderful musicians. And I got lots of experience and training playing with them."

Marion pointed to a photograph of the great cellist Pablo Casals and said, "He was one of my idols." Marion was chosen to appear under the master at the historic "Salud Casals" on April 15, 1970, in Philharmonic Hall at Lincoln Center, joining leading cellists from around the world.

While Marion was playing, Clarissa was planning. When Everett Lee started his Cosmopolitan Little Symphony twenty-nine years ago, Clarissa was on the board. She was also part of the committee of fifty women who spent much of their spare time raising funds for the orchestra.

Of her present activities, Clarissa said, "Two loves have I —the Symphony of the New World and Triad." For its twelve years of existence, she has served on the board and been co-chairman of the Manhattan-Bronx Friends. And she and Marion were the founders of Triad.

She explained her commitment to the Symphony as follows: "Personally, I was very much involved because I knew from experience what Marion and other musicians of his caliber had gone through. They never had opportunities to play with the major orchestras simply because they were Black."

Clarissa founded Triad because "there was no other organization that I knew of that was providing opportunities for Black artists to be heard downtown to get the critical notices so vital to help them further their careers." Since 1971, Triad has presented an annual series at Alice Tully Hall.

When I left the Cumbos' apartment that evening, I knew

that we had only shared a few paragraphs of a living history of the Black contribution to the musical life of New York. Still stored away in their memory bank, in those photographs and boxes of yellowed clippings, was enough material for a book.[2]

63 Clyde Turner's Cultural Garden

For almost two decades, Clyde S. Turner has put together a musical entertainment to barnstorm around the country. He has cultivated a kind of cultural garden where many of our finest vocal talents have been given the opportunity to blossom.

On Sunday afternoon, May 30, 1976 at Mother A.M.E. Zion, he offered a bouquet of his choicest talents. Included were Miriam Burton, LeRoy Broadwith, Delores Davis, Janette Moody, Robert Mosely, Lorna Myers, Dianne Randolph, Louise Rosebrooks, and George Tipton.

The highlight of the program was a scene from Gershwin's *Porgy and Bess* featuring Robert Mosely, Delores Davis, Miriam Burton, and Janette Moody as Porgy, Bess, Serena, and the Strawberry Woman, respectively. They are all superb singing actors and they made the scene live.

Another very special moment was the aria "Martern aller Arten" from *The Abduction From the Seraglio* by Mozart (Act II), sung by Miss Moody. She revealed a powerful, marvelously controlled coloratura voice of the first rank.

This program was listed as a "Three-Fold Musical Afternoon," a memorial to Mrs. Jamesena Walker and Paul Robeson and a Bicentennial salute. It was also a tribute to Turner himself, a man who has earned a very special place in the hearts of the musical community.[3]

VIII

ATTITUDES

64 The Critic and His Cat

One day, as I sat down to begin my weekly column, my handsome cat, Kukla, refused to move from his comfortable resting place on the desk and gave me the evil eye. He asked, "Daddy, what is music criticism all about?"

In my most daddy-like tones, I explained: "A music critic is a kind of thermometer. Using his own background as a guide, he sets certain standards for a performance. Then he sits quietly at a concert and lets the mercury of his mind rise or fall to a certain mark on the scale."

"But, Daddy, do you really think that I am naive enough to believe that you critics are that pure?" asked Kukla. "I've read some reviews that have ruined the careers of certain performers. Take that critic who waged a battle with Dimitri Mitropoulos and finally succeeded in getting the Philharmonic to change conductors?"

I answered, "That's one of the dangers. Sometimes the critic begins to feel like the Lord and goes beyond the call of duty. The public is amused, because critics often use wit as a weapon, not sensing what is at stake."

Kukla then asked, "Can you show me one example of a critic doing good?"

Taking a copy of *Schumann on Music and Musicians* (edited by Konrad Wolff, New York: Pantheon, 1946) off my shelf, I showed Kukla an article written by the famous German composer and critic that heralded the arrival of a new musical genius—Johannes Brahms. "As a critic, Schumann was able to help launch the career of a young man in whom he believed."

"You must be getting old," Kukla said. "You told me before that a critic is a thermometer whose job it is to gauge a musical performance. You didn't say anything about press agentry as one of the duties."

I answered, "Perhaps I should have made it clear that I meant that in connection with reviews of a specific performance. I also believe that the critic has other responsibilities to his readers, too. He should encourage new personalities who appear to perpetuate the highest standards in their art. He should discourage those who do not seem to have talent."

Kukla interrupted, "Okay, Daddy, I get the picture. We could talk about this all night long, but I'm tired. But before I go to bed, I'd like you to read this little poem by Paul Laurence Dunbar:"

> Dear critic, who my lightness so deplores,
> Would I might study to be prince of bores,
> Right wisely would I rule that dull estate—
> But, sir, I may not, till you abdicate.[1]

As I look over this article from my early days as a music critic, I am reminded of the pioneers who have paved the way. One of these was Nora Douglas Holt (1895–1974), critic of the *Amsterdam News* for many years and the only Black member of the New York Music Critics Circle.

Dr. Gladys Graham, whose syndicated column informed Black America of its musical activities, was on the board of the Music Critics Association. Like Miss Holt, she encouraged my early journalistic endeavors. Miss Graham died in 1976.

For many years, William Duncan Allen wrote a column in the *Oakland Post* (California). Other important Black critics include Dean Robert Nolan of the *Michigan Chronicle* (Detroit), Earl Calloway of the *Chicago Defender*, and Charles Theodore Stone of the *New Crusader* (Chicago).

As far as I know, only two Black critics have held posts on the staff of white newspapers. Collins George has only recently retired as music critic of the *Detroit Free Press*. The gifted young composer Carman Moore has been a frequent contributor to the *Village Voice*, a New York weekly.

Outside of the United States, Durrell Echols has worked as a music critic on the staff of *Abendzeitung* in Munich, where he has lived for twenty years. Echols, who was born in Washington, D.C., assisted Gerhard Huesch in his classes as a diction coach.

65   The Relevance of Classical Music

During my first year as music reviewer for the *Amsterdam News*, I received a number of letters from readers. One of the subjects that comes up most often is the question of the relevance of classical music to the Black experience.

In the introduction to my book *Famous Black Entertainers*

of Today (New York: Dodd, Mead, 1974), I noted that a large number of Black musicians have chosen to specialize in the area of European classical music. I also commented that it was unfortunate that so little had been written about them.

I pointed to the great violinist George Bridegtower (1779–1860) for whom Beethoven was supposed to have written and dedicated his celebrated *Kreutzer* Sonata. He was born in Poland of an African father and a European mother and was a favorite in the highest musical circles of Europe.

Another violin virtuoso was the Cuban-born Joseph White (1839–1920). Although Europe was the scene of most of his triumphs, White did play in the United States (Boston and New York) in 1875. A few years ago, the Symphony of the New World revived his little-known Violin Concerto.

One of the best answers to the question of the relevance of European classical music came from conductor James De Preist during one of our conversations. He is the musical director of L'Orchestre Symphonique de Quebec, a post to which he has only recently been appointed.

He told me: "The first experience is the human experience which transcends race. Pain, happiness, depression, exultation—all of the basic human emotions that have nothing to do with race—are affected by music. The Black experience adds a special character to all of this.

"The way I show *my* grief or anger will be different, but they are fundamental human emotions and these are the emotions that I try to have the music touch and convey *that* to audiences. In that sense, classical music is relevant to anyone who wants to give himself over to it." [2]

66   A Grave Affair

News Item—Representative Frank Chelf (D—Ky) told his House colleagues last week that he has received hundreds of letters supporting his stand against tampering with the lyrics of Stephen Foster's "My Old Kentucky Home." The AGE music critic, Raoul Abdul, immediately contacted the composer, deceased for ninety-four years, through a noted Harlem medium to get the composer's reaction.

Abdul: Is that you, Mr. Foster?

Foster: (In a muffled voice) I've been dead these ninety years, and no one has disturbed my peace. What do you want?

Abdul: Did you know that Representative Chelf of Kentucky is campaigning to keep the words of "My Old Kentucky Home" intact in spite of the fact that many Negroes are offended by some of them?

Foster: No, we don't get much current news up here. But I suppose you want to know what I think about it all. If the darkies are offended, then why don't they change the words?

Abdul: (Offended) Mr. Foster, it's the word *darkies* that offends us.

Foster: I see. When I was on earth it wasn't offensive to use the word *darkies*. It was used most affectionately. I keep forgetting that times have changed, what with the NAACP and equal rights, and sometimes the old word slips out.

Abdul: Would you change the words if you were on earth today?

Foster: Of course! I would choose words that suited the times, and I certainly wouldn't want to offend anyone. Now, Mr. Abdul, may I ask you a big favor?

Abdul: Of course, sir.

Foster: Next time, please don't call me. I'll call you.[3]

67   A Nod to Black Creativity

Shortly before the New York Philharmonic embarked on its recent six-week tour of Europe and the United States, conductor emeritus Leonard Bernstein held a press conference. He noted with pride that most of the composers chosen for this series of all-American programs were of Jewish background.

At its Bicentennial concert in Central Park on Sunday evening, July 4th, 1976, the orchestra capped its tour with a program that celebrated the Jewish contribution to the musical life of America. The composers were William Schuman, Bernstein himself, Aaron Copland, and George Gershwin.

The program opened with Schuman's *American Festival* Overture, which following its premiere in 1939 by Koussevitzsky, helped launch the career of this composer, which culminated in his being appointed president of Lincoln Center. This athletic work, built on variants of a three-note motive, was "festive."

Orchestrated by Sid Ramin, Irwin Kostal, and Bernstein, a series of "Symphonic Dances" from *West Side Story*, provided a kind of tribute to Puerto Rican life in New York. The lovely section based on "Somewhere," played against a back-drop of the New York skyline, wove a spine-tingling magical spell.

Although it is not especially distinctive, Copland's *A Lincoln Portrait* (1942) was given a moving performance with William Warfield narrating the text based on Lincoln's own words. A breakdown in sound equipment did not cause this veteran artist to lose his cool.

A nod to the musical contributions of Black America was provided second-handed by the inclusion of Gershwin's *Rhapsody in Blue* and *An American in Paris*. It is now history that Gershwin took Black jazz and blues, added touches of urban Jewish Tin Pan Alley, and came up with something original.

Bernstein both conducted and acted as soloist in the *Rhapsody*. Despite a few missed notes here and there, he brought out nuances that gave the performance distinction of the kind that remains unsurpassed when an artist is in his own element.

The familiar *An American in Paris* brought this festive concert to a rousing conclusion. The orchestra never sounded better, even with artificial amplification. Yes, it was a fine tribute to the ethnic roots of New York with a slight nod to Black American creativity.[4]

This was an odd program to have taken to Europe as a Bicentennial salute. Here, the Black contribution to our musical culture is only seen through white eyes—namely Gershwin and Bernstein. It shows again that there may be some truth in the charge that Bernstein would rather have a Black Panther in his living room than on one of his programs.

68   Was it the Fish or the Question?

Did Miss Alice Tully choke on the fish? Or, was it my question?

The scene was a fashionable restaurant where the Chamber Music Society of Lincoln Center held a luncheon press conference on Wednesday, April 28, 1976, to announce "interesting new aspects of the 1976–77 season."

When I arrived dressed in my new gray flannel suit, I was greeted by press representative Miss Alix B. Williamson, who introduced me to our hostess, Chairman of the Board Miss Tully. The latter, a handsome woman in control of cultural purse strings, smiled warmly and then gazed into outer space. Alice Tully Hall was named for her.

Would I like a drink? asked Miss Williamson as she led me to the bar and handed me a press kit. After ordering a plain ginger ale, I proceeded to peruse a list of the composers of the 373 works played by the Society since 1969. (I made a mental note that there were no Blacks included.)

After a short time, my colleagues from the press gathered, and we sat down to hear words of welcome from Miss Tully, President Edward R. Wardwell, Artistic Director Charles Wadsworth, and Executive Director Norman Singer. It was all just as polite and charming as one could wish.

We learned that next season the Society was adding violinist James Buswell to its permanent ensemble. Schubert and Schumann would be honored with a survey of their chamber works. And among the sixty-one events offered by the Society, works by a number of American composers would be included.

While these tidbits of incidental intelligence were being imparted, I scanned a list of guest artists who had appeared with the group. Since 1969, two Blacks had been included, pianist Andre Watts and violist Marcus Thompson. (Again I made a mental note of this fact.)

My ears pricked up when I heard Mr. Wadsworth ask if there were any questions from the press. I politely held up my hand and simply asked how I could justify telling *Amsterdam News* readers about a series that, since 1969, had not included any Black composers and only two instrumentalists.

Icy silence followed.

Mr. Wardwell proceeded to make some remark to the effect that the Society was indeed not racist (no one suggested it) and that its concern was purely artistic.

Were there any Black composers who met their standards?

I mentioned Howard Swanson, who won the 1952 Music Critics Circle Award as best composer.

Mr. Wadsworth interrupted and said that he had some manuscripts of William Grant Still, but had not yet played through them. (Mr. Wadsworth was unknown until he played for Shirley Verrett. I wondered if he had forgotten his Black friends so soon.)

In any case, Mr. Wadsworth said that if I would supply him with a list of outstanding Black composers and performers, he would give them due consideration.

We were informed that lunch was getting cold, so we repaired to the dining area. On the way to the table, I thought to myself, We'll see.

Did Miss Tully choke on the fish—or my question?

More important: Does Miss Alice Tully know that she is being manipulated into using her money and name to help cultural projects that might turn her into a symbol of white racism in music?[5]

When this article appeared on the front page of the *Amsterdam News*, May 8, 1976, there was great rejoicing on the part of many Black composers and instrumentalists. Lincoln Center reacted in another way. One officer accused me of insulting Miss Tully, the musical benefactress.

Nothing could be further from the truth. Any intelligent reader could see that she was only used as a *symbol* of money and power on the musical scene. The final paragraph poses a very serious question for which all the Miss Tullys of the country must find an answer.

From the very beginning, Blacks have felt alienated from the musical life at Lincoln Center. Every effort to affect change has been met with indifference on the part of its officers. They claim that artistic competence, not race, is their only consideration.

A look at the facts proves otherwise. In 1969, two Black musicians—Earl Madison (cellist) and Arthur D. Davis (double-bassist)—charged the New York Philharmonic with racism in its hiring policies. The New York City Commission on Human Rights conducted a series of hearings on the case.

The Philharmonic was found both guilty and not guilty. It was found not guilty on the main charge of discrimination in terms of permanent hiring, but guilty regarding the hiring of substitute and extra players. Shortly after, it engaged several Black guest conductors and instrumental soloists.

Three years after the hearings, the orchestra and the commission finally agreed on a long-range plan to insure minority-group musicians equal employment opportunities in the Philharmonic. It was agreed that the commission would review progress of this plan until 1974.

After that time, there was no longer what was in effect a watchdog in this matter and the Philharmonic reverted to its old policies. On its regular subscription series, there were no Black members of the orchestra, no Black composers, no Black guest conductors, and only one token Andre Watts as an instrumental soloist.

I am convinced that the only solution to the problem of racism in classical music is for responsible citizens of all races to demand that grants from public funds such as The National Endowment for the Arts be withheld from all institutions that do not meet the needs of the *entire* community.

Notes

I COMPOSERS

1. *New York Age*, February 21, 1959
2. *Amsterdam News*, July 17, 1976
3. *Amsterdam News*, February 21, 1976
4. Associated Negro Press, June 7, 1975
5. *Amsterdam News*, February 12, 1977
6. *Amsterdam News*, February 12, 1977
7. *Amsterdam News*, May 8, 1976
8. *Amsterdam News*, May 1, 1976
9. *Amsterdam News*, March 5, 1977
10. *Amsterdam News*, February 19, 1977
11. *Amsterdam News*, February 26, 1977
12. *Amsterdam News*, June 12, 1976
13. *Amsterdam News*, February 14, 1976
14. *New York Courier*, August 29, 1964
15. *Amsterdam News*, February 5, 1977
16. *Amsterdam News*, April 3, 1976
17. *Amsterdam News*, March 19, 1977

II SINGERS

1. Associated Negro Press, November 13, 1965
2. Associated Negro Press, April 24, 1965
3. *Amsterdam News*, January 31, 1976
4. *Cleveland Call and Post*, July 29, 1950

5. Associated Negro Press, October 16, 1965
6. *Amsterdam News*, September 18, 1976
7. *Amsterdam News*, January 29, 1977
8. *Amsterdam News*, May 15, 1976
9. *Amsterdam News*, December 4, 1976
10. *Amsterdam News*, April 17, 1976

III OPERAS AND OPERA COMPANIES

1. *Amsterdam News*, February 14, 1976
2. *Amsterdam News*, September 25, 1976
3. Associated Negro Press, March 3, 1973
4. *Amsterdam News*, October 2, 1976
5. *Amsterdam News*, July 31, 1976
6. *Amsterdam News*, April 10, 1976

IV KEYBOARD ARTISTS

1. *New York Age*, June 27, 1959
2. Associated Negro Press, December 2, 1972
3. *Amsterdam News*, February 7, 1976
4. *Amsterdam News*, October 9, 1971

V INSTRUMENTALISTS

1. *Amsterdam News*, March 27, 1976
2. *Amsterdam News*, June 5, 1976

VI CONDUCTORS, ORCHESTRAS AND CHORUSES

1. *Amsterdam News*, January 24, 1976
2. *Amsterdam News*, November 6, 1976
3. *Amsterdam News*, October 30, 1976
4. Associated Negro Press, May 17, 1964
5. *Amsterdam News*, June 19, 1976

VII DIVERTISSEMENTS

1. *New York Age*, October 18, 1958
2. *Amsterdam News*, July 31, 1976
3. *Amsterdam News*, June 19, 1976

VIII ATTITUDES

1. *New York Age*, August 9, 1958
2. *Amsterdam News*, January 22, 1977
3. *New York Age*, (Month Unmarked), 1958
4. *Amsterdam News*, July 10, 1976
5. *Amsterdam News*, May 8, 1976

SOME OTHER NOTABLE MUSICAL EVENTS

1839   Frank Johnson, conductor of an all-Black military band in Philadelphia, adds a string section to play classical music— possibly the first Black concert orchestra.

1870   Premiere of *Il Guarany* by the Mulatto Brazilian composer Carlos Gomes at La Scala, Milan; the U.S. premiere was at the Star Theatre in New York in 1884.

1871   First tour of the Fisk Jubilee Singers.

1892   Sissieretta Jones (Black Patti), after appearing in the Negro Jubilee at Madison Square Garden and giving two recitals at the Academy of Music, is invited to the White House by President Benjamin Harrison.

1893   Joseph Douglass, violinist, performs at the Chicago World's Fair; later he performs for Presidents McKinley and Taft and makes recordings for the Victor Talking Machine Co.

1896   Luranah Aldridge, contralto and daughter of Ira Aldridge, sings at the Bayreuth Festival.

1902   *The Negro Musical Journal* begins publication, lasts less than two years.

1912   First Carnegie Hall concert by the Clef Club Orchestra of 125 led by James Reese Europe.

1912   Raymond Augustus Lawson, pianist, is soloist with the Hartford Philharmonic.

1915   Melville Charlton becomes the first Black member of the American Guild of Organists.

1917   Harry T. Burleigh, singer, accompanist, composer and the first to arrange spirituals for solo voice and piano, wins the National Association of Colored People's Spingarn Medal.

1917   Nora Holt's *Music and Poetry* begins four years of publication.

1920   E. Gilbert Anderson organizes and conducts the Harlem Symphony Orchestra; earlier he had established the Philadelphia Negro Symphony.

1921   The first Black recording company, best known for the Black Swan label, is established in New York.

1921   Helen Hagan, pianist, at Aeolian Hall, the first Black pianist to play in a major New York concert hall.

1924   The New York recital debut of Jules Bledsoe, baritone, at Aeolian Hall.

1927   The Rodman Wanamaker Prize for works by Black composers is established; among the winners are Carl Diton, Hall Johnson and J. Harold Brown.

1927   Abbie Mitchell, soprano, sings at Steinway Hall in New York.

1931   Edward Matthews, baritone, presented by Roland Hayes, at Town Hall.

1935   Flora Thompson is the first Black pianist to give a Town Hall recital.

1938   A newly-formed Harlem Symphony, conducted by Wen Talbert, director of the Works Progress Administration Project, performs at the Lafayette Theatre.

1939   Penelope Johnson, violinist, makes her Town Hall debut.

1940   Town Hall debut of Aubrey Pankey, baritone.

1941   New York recital debut of Kenneth Spencer, bass.

1942 Town Hall debut of Thomasina Talley, pianist.

1944 Town Hall debut of Portia White, contralto, "the Canadian Marian Anderson."

1945 Rudolph Dunbar conducts the first performance after V-E Day by the Berlin Philharmonic.

1945 George Walker, known later as a composer, in his Town Hall debut as a pianist.

1946 Town Hall debut of Helen Thipgen, soprano.

1948 Lawrence Winters, who was Lawrence Whisonant when he sang with the National Negro Opera Company, makes his debut with the New York City Opera in *Aida* and in 1951 becomes the first Black to sing *Rigoletto*.

1950 Lois Towles, pianist, in her Town Hall debut.

1951 Rawn Spearman, tenor, in his Town Hall debut; later sang as a baritone.

1952 Alyne Dumas Lee, soprano, in her Town Hall debut, beginning a short but brilliant career.

1954 Pianist Eugene Haynes makes his Town Hall debut followed four years later by a much-acclaimed Carnegie Hall recital.

1954 Martha Flowers, soprano, wins the Naumburg Award and makes her Town Hall debut.

1954 Charlotte Holloman, soprano, makes her Town Hall debut.

1955 Vivian Scott, pianist, in her Town Hall debut as winner of the Just Us Good Guys (J.U.G.G.) Award.

1955 Clarence Cameron White, veteran violinist, conductor and composer, wins the Benjamin Award for his "Elegy."

1955 Everett Lee conducts a performance of *La Traviata* by New York City Center Opera, the first Black to conduct a major American opera company.

1955 Charles Holland, tenor, who made his recital debut at Town Hall in 1940, triumphs at the Opéra-Comique in Paris as Nadir in Bizet's *The Pearl Fishers*.

1957 Donald White, cellist, becomes a member of the Cleveland Orchestra.

1958 Matthew Kennedy, pianist, makes his New York debut at Carnegie Recital Hall.

1959 Raymond Jackson, pianist, winner of the J.U.G.G. Award, in Town Hall debut.

1960 Town Hall debut of pianist Armenta Adams.

1963 Seth McCoy becomes soloist with the Robert Shaw Chorale; since then he has sung with almost every major American orchestra and is currently with the Bach Aria Group.

1965 Metropolitan Opera debut of Felicia Weathers as Lisa in Tchaikowsky's *The Queen of Spades*.

1966 Simon Estes, bass baritone, and Veronica Tyler, soprano, are winners in the First International Tchaikowsky Vocal Competition in Moscow.

1966 Metropolitan Opera debut of Reri Grist as Rosina in *The Barber of Seville*.

1967 All-Lieder recital by baritone Raoul Abdul and pianist John Wustman at Carnegie Recital Hall.

1969 Andrew Frierson, baritone, becomes Director of the Henry Street Settlement Music School.

1970 Baltimore Lyric Theatre with the Baltimore Symphony and Morgan State College Choir conducted by Everett Lee performs *Till Victory Is Won*, an opera by Mark Fax with libretto by Owen Dodson.

1970 Lola Hayes, prominent voice teacher, becomes the first Black president of the New York Singing Teachers Association.

1972 World premiere of *A Musical Service for Louis* by Roger Dickerson by the New Orleans Philharmonic.

1972 Nerine Barrett plays Beethoven's Second Piano Concerto with the New York Philharmonic, the first Black pianist to appear on the regular subscription series.

1972 Robert Jordan, pianist, in a debut recital at Alice Tully Hall.

1972 Louise Parker, contralto, appears in the National Educational Television world premiere of *The Trial of Mary Lincoln*, as well as recital and orchestral engagements here and abroad.

1973 Ronald Lipscomb, cellist, makes his Alice Tully Hall debut under the auspices of Triad Presentations, Inc.

1974 Elayne Jones, tympanist who joined the San Francisco Symphony in 1972, is denied tenure by vote of the all-white players committee of the orchestra in spite of praise by critics and leading musicians.

1974 Leon Bates plays the Bartók Third Piano Concerto with the Philadelphia Orchestra under Eugene Ormandy.

1974 Soprano Veronica Tyler, who had sung leading roles with the New York City Opera, makes her recital debut in Alice Tully Hall.

1975 Samuel Dilworth-Leslie plays a program of the piano music of Gabriel Fauré at Carnegie Recital Hall.

1975 The New York Philharmonic under Pierre Boulez plays premiere of "Wildfires and Field Songs" composed by Carman Moore on a $10,000 commission from the orchestra in association with the New York State Council on the Arts.

1975 Frances Walker, pianist, performs a program entirely by Black composers at Carnegie Recital Hall.

1976 Elwyn Adams, violinist, makes his first New York appearance with an orchestra, the Symphony of the New World.

1977   Dedication of the permanent home of the Harlem School of the Arts, founded and directed by Dorothy Maynor.

1977   The Schubert Society, founded in 1927 by Edward H. Margetson, organist, choirmaster and composer, presents its Golden Jubilee concert in his memory at the American Academy and Institute of Arts and Letters.

1977   Hilda Harris, mezzo soprano, makes her Metropolitan Opera debut in Berg's *Lulu*; earlier she had appeared with the New York City Opera and as a recitalist.

1977   New York Philharmonic Festival: A Celebration of Black Composers with conductors Paul Freeman and Leon Thompson.

Index

DATE DUE